POP ACADEMY

Sexual and Reproductive Health and Rights

A Multicountry Study on Self-care in Young People

Contributors
Ash Pachauri
Drishya Pathak
Komal Mittal
Nahid Perez Ayala
Norma Patricia Muñoz Sevilla
Philo Magdalene
Saroj Pachauri

Cover Design
Harun Ahmed

First edition

This book was professionally typeset on Reedsy.
Find out more at reedsy.com

Contents

Foreword

Self-care interventions are among the most promising and exciting new approaches to improving health and wellbeing, placing people at the center of care and allowing individuals to be agents of their own health. The expanding array of self-care products and practices is beginning to reshape the way health care is delivered, and the ways in which individuals seek care. At the same time, a large and diverse youth population is in need of and is seeking sexual and reproductive health information and services. This convergence makes this an ideal moment to examine the role of self-care among adolescents and youth in diverse settings and contexts. The book, *Sexual and Reproductive Health and Right of Young People: A Multicountry Study on Self-care* aim to do just that. Dedicated to exploring the attitudes, beliefs, and practices of young people in India, Mexico, Nigeria, and the United States, the authors provide insights and evidence around the ways in which young people conceptualize self-care and the actions they take. The authors dedicate a chapter to each of the countries, providing in-depth country and context specific learnings. The authors analyze the attitudes, practices, behaviors, and experiences with self-care technologies such as oral contraceptives and self-injectables for family planning, mifepristone for abortion, and pre-and post-exposure prophylaxis for HIV prevention. Further they explore the gender dimension of each in different settings.

While country specific themes emerge, overall, the authors conclude that self-care interventions must be systematically implemented to promote sexual and reproductive health and rights of young people and highlight the need for a supportive policy environment to enhance the adoption of self-care practices for sexual and reproductive health and rights.

This book is important reading for a broad audience of program designers, implementers, civil society actors, researchers, and all those supporting the development of self-care intention for adolescents and youth in the SRHR arena.

Dr. Martha Brady
Senior Technical Advisor for Women's Health and Self-Care

Foreword

I write a note of appreciation to the authors of this book because research has shown that contributions in the area of self-care for sexual and reproductive health are critical for improving equity and efficiency. If Universal Health Care is our goal and if we believe that health is an entitlement and a right, then well conceptualized efforts are needed to promote self-care, and enable people to manage their health in ways that are often beyond the reach of health systems. This book offers a compassionate and informative roadmap for individuals seeking to navigate the complexities of sexual and reproductive health programs. Through this book, Dr. Saroj Pachauri acknowledges the intrinsic power individuals possess to manage their wellbeing. It is a powerful assertion that healthcare is not solely the domain of medical professionals, but a collaborative process shared by individuals and medical providers.

Facts and figures tell the story. The World Health Organization (WHO) estimates that about 4.3 billion people have insufficient access to basic healthcare facilities and services. By 2030, it is estimated that the world will be short of 18 million healthcare workers to meet the Universal Health Coverage (UHC) goals. Furthermore, ongoing humanitarian crises, climate change, pandemics such as COVID-19, and political conflicts are adversely impacting the global reach of healthcare products and services, leading to poor health conditions in affected regions. The new and emerging world order that is seeing these phenomena across the globe be it famines in Africa, conflicts in Ukraine and Palestine, pandemics caused by mutating viruses across the globe, increasing numbers of forcibly displaced populations, and diminishing numbers of productive age groups in the demographic profile of many continents, makes this book timely and contemporary.

The need for self-care initiatives is equally relevant and pertinent in countries where young people, especially adolescents, form more than 60 percent of the demographic profile like India. It is now well understood that adolescents need access to self-care especially in the area of sexual and reproductive health because access to such services is tainted with barriers like provider attitudes that create a huge social distance between the provider and the client. Seeking services related to contraception, safe abortion, and the prevention of sexually transmitted infections including HIV/AIDS can be quite traumatic for young people, especially in the age group of 10-14 years. Findings show that while adolescent girls may have knowledge of abortion in general, they lack specific knowledge of the sources of care and, therefore, delay care-seeking. Access to care is also challenged due to the fear of stigma, lack of resources, and provider bias. Efforts have been made by a number of agencies to reduce the distance by engaging service providers in self-examining their attitudes to sex and sexuality in order to create safe spaces for seekers of services. Building their self-esteem is also being used to enable better access. In fact, self-care practices have the potential to reduce the pressure on healthcare systems by encouraging people of all ages to take active ownership of their health. The emphasis of this book on the intersectionality of sexual and reproductive health with other social determinants of health such as gender, socioeconomic status, and cultural beliefs, provides a holistic perspective that is essential for effective self-care.

Self-care in sexual and reproductive health is not just about physical health, it is also about recognizing the autonomy and agency of young people. It can help them to advocate for themselves and for their communities. It can challenge societal norms and expectations that restrict people's potential and, thereby, develop their self-worth and confidence. Several quality self-care interventions for sexual and reproductive health and rights (SRHR) are already available in many settings. Others are being rapidly introduced, such as self-injectable contraception and self-sampling kits for the human papilloma virus (HPV).

As with all healthcare interventions, the way in which self-care initiatives are financed and managed is key to their success. Self-care should not be seen as a replacement for sustainable and high-quality health services. Even though self-care may be the only care available in some circumstances, such as in humanitarian crises, there is a tangible difference between empowering and supporting individuals to manage their own health and simply passing on the healthcare burdens of cost and service delivery to individuals. Therefore, a crucial step needed is to reorient health systems so that the responsibility for supporting self-care is integral to health systems. Healthcare should be co-produced with individuals and communities. Unhelpful or harmful self-care practices should be identified and people using them supported with safer alternatives.

I congratulate the authors of this book for undertaking research in several countries to strengthen self-care practices. Qualitative research has been undertaken in Mexico on high school students and college graduates (married and unmarried) to study their motivations for using self-care. In India, the authors have examined young people's attitudes, practices, and behaviors regarding self-care interventions. This knowledge can be used to highlight the need for a supportive environment to enhance self-care for SRHR so that these services can be integrated successfully into mainstream healthcare systems in the country. Similar explorations by the authors in the United States of America have highlighted that there is a significant research gap on SRH self-care practices among young people in the USA. Addressing this gap is crucial for developing effective interventions and improving the quality of services. The discourse in Nigeria is based on an examination of the gender differences in existing attitudes, practices, and experiences with self-care technologies such as oral contraceptives and self-injectables for family planning, mifepristone for abortion, and pre-and post-exposure prophylaxis for HIV prevention.

This research, will no doubt, strengthen the existing responses to self-care. As we digitalize globally, the speed of access to self-care technologies will improve. The associated risks of these technologies will be better understood and the spectrum of the benefits of self-care will promote gains in young people. This book is a significant contribution to the field of self-care for sexual and reproductive health of young people. It is a valuable resource for healthcare providers, policy-makers, educators, and community leaders. I am confident that this book will inspire and inform countless individuals.

Madhu Bala Nath
Member Governing Board
Population Services International

Preface

People have practiced self-care for millennia, but in recent years, new products, information, and technologies have transformed how health services are delivered. The traditional provider-to-receiver model in many health systems must now be complemented by a self-care approach to empower people to prevent, test for, and treat diseases independently. This shift is essential to achieving universal health coverage (UHC), which promotes a people-centered approach where individuals actively manage their health rather than being passive recipients of care. Health literacy plays a vital role in this, enabling individuals to make informed decisions using evidence-based self-care interventions, especially in areas like sexuality and reproduction.

This book presents the findings of a multicountry study on the sexual and reproductive health and rights (SRHR) of high school students and college graduates (married and unmarried) in Mexico, India, the USA, and Nigeria. The review highlights a serious paucity of research on self-care in SRHR among young people in these regions, emphasizing the need for further investigation to develop effective programs. With at least half of the world's population lacking access to essential health services, self-care interventions are crucial to complementing the formal health system.

This book will engage a global audience, including policy-makers, program implementers, academics, donors, and health activists.

Acknowledgments

We thank the World Health Organization (WHO) for its invaluable support for this study. The WHO's guidance and encouragement have been instrumental in shaping this work, and we deeply appreciate its continued commitment to advancing knowledge in self-care and its impact on sexual and reproductive health and rights among young people globally.

We sincerely thank Dr. Manjulaa Narasimhan, Acting Unit Head of Sexual Health and Well-being across the Life Course, for her insightful leadership, unwavering support, and expert guidance throughout this research. Her dedication to advancing sexual and reproductive health and rights has provided vital inspiration for this study, and her contributions to self-care as a global health priority continue to shape meaningful progress in the field.

We are grateful to all individuals and organizations that contributed to this work. Their collective efforts have made this study possible.

Rationale for Self-Care Study, Study Objectives, and Study Methodology

Background

The World Health Organization's working definition of self-care includes *"the ability of individuals, families and, communities to promote health, prevent disease, maintain health, and cope with illness and disability with or without the support of a healthcare provider."* (1). While this definition covers all aspects of self-care, the focus of this book is on self-care for sexual and reproductive health and rights (SRHR) of young people.

There has been a growing interest in self-care in recent years because of the diverse pressures on the health service system, including depersonalized medical care, the high cost of technology, the focus on curative care, the increase in knowledge of self-care by lay people, and recognition of the limits of medical care.

People have been practicing self-care for millennia. However, in recent years, new products, information, and technologies have changed how health services are delivered. The provider-to-receiver model that is at the core of many health systems must be complemented with a self-care model through which people can be empowered to prevent, test for, and treat diseases themselves. This would propel efforts towards achieving universal health coverage (UHC). UHC is a people-centered approach that views people as active decision-makers in their own health and not merely as passive recipients of health services. A people-centered approach supports health literacy so that people can understand health issues and can take charge of their own health using evidence-based self-care interventions. When people have agency and autonomy, they can make and enact decisions in all aspects of their lives, including in relation to sexuality and reproduction.

People use self-care interventions for many reasons. Individuals may choose a self-care health intervention for reasons of convenience, cost, empowerment, or when it provides a better fit with their values and lifestyles. Proven efficacy and endorsement by the health system may be another reason to choose self-care interventions. Given that an ideal, well-functioning health system is seldom a reality, particularly in resource-constrained settings, individuals may also opt for self-care interventions in order to avoid the health system because of its poor-quality services or because information, interventions, or products are inappropriate, unaffordable, or inaccessible. Stigma from the healthcare system and from families and communities is another reason why people turn to self-care. Self-care interventions fulfill a particularly important role in these situations as the alternative might be no access at all to health interventions (2).

The conceptual framework of self-care acknowledges that while there have always been traditional self-care practices, people are now accessing new information and products through a variety of channels, including pharmacies and the Internet. Recent years have witnessed a phenomenal increase in mobile technologies and digital health for self-care. An enabling policy and legal environment is an essential prerequisite for implementing safe and high-quality self-care interventions (2).

Some self-care interventions, such as condoms, are fully controlled by the individual. Others require interaction with the health service system. For example, HIV self-testing requires confirmation by the health system.

Today, at least half of the world's population does not have access to essential health services. Therefore, there is a clear rationale for implementing self-care interventions to complement services provided by the formal health system.

WHO guideline on sexual and reproductive health and rights

In 2019, WHO issued a guideline on sexual and reproductive health self-care interventions. The guideline addresses a wide range of issues, including antenatal care, childbirth, postpartum and newborn care, family planning, safe abortion, sexually transmitted infections (STIs), including HIV, and sexual health. The purpose of the guideline is to provide people-centered, evidence-based guidance to individuals, communities, and countries to promote quality health services and self-care interventions within public health strategies. Evidence-based self-care recommended by WHO includes information on sexual and reproductive health issues as well as on ways in which individuals can obtain drugs and devices. Many diagnostic and digital products can be used with or without the direct supervision of a healthcare provider. Some examples are self-injectable contraceptives, self-sampling kits, and HIV self-tests (3).

Authors' earlier research on self-care

There is a severe paucity of research on self-care globally. Research was conducted in India in the year 2019 to understand the knowledge, perceptions, and barriers of four vulnerable communities, including men who have sex with men (MSM), transgender, female sex workers (FSWs), and long-distance truck drivers. Research questions addressed their perceptions and experience with self-care, their sources of information, their motivations for using self-care, the barriers they encountered, and the mechanisms they employed when self-care failed. Quotes were generously used to amplify the voices of the members of these marginalized and vulnerable communities. Research results were supplemented with personal narratives of the community members, which provided invaluable insights into their lived experiences.

These case studies discussed the evolution of self-care interventions and their impact on the health of the community, in particular on sexual and reproductive health and HIV prevention. They also included a discussion on reproductive rights, which are seriously violated in these communities. Issues related to stigma and discrimination and violence among these communities were highlighted. Finally, factors that resulted in changes in policies and programs to improve their sexual and reproductive health and grant them the right to health, education, and employment were discussed. The case studies provide an understanding of what worked and what did not work in mobilizing and empowering these vulnerable communities (4).

Study objectives

A multicountry study was conducted in seven states in India, five in Mexico, six in Nigeria, and six in the USA.

The objectives of the study were:

1. To examine the knowledge, attitudes, and practices of high school students and college graduates (married and unmarried) on self-care interventions for sexual and reproductive health and rights.

2. To analyze their attitudes, practices and behaviors with respect to oral contraceptives for family planning, misoprostol for abortion management, pre- and post-exposure prophylaxis for HIV prevention, and other self-care technologies for sexual and reproductive health and rights

3. To assess the relationship of gender and self-care interventions for sexual and reproductive health and rights in the context of the COVID-19 pandemic.

Study methodology

Data was collected using qualitative research methods. The subjectivity of qualitative research leads to various procedural problems and research biases. This method of research is time-consuming, but it can draw out information on sensitive issues.

The interviews were conducted online and in person. In-depth interviews (IDIs), focus group discussions (FGDs), and key informant interviews (KIIs) were conducted. Values, preferences, and practices of these communities about self-care for sexual and reproductive health and HIV prevention were assessed. The aim was to understand their self-care practices, their motivations for using self-care interventions, and the challenges they faced in adopting self-care, including addressing social, economic, and mental barriers.

Challenges faced and addressed

Initially, when this self-care research study was designed, its scope covered countries such as Cameroon, Egypt, Uganda, Nigeria, Mexico, India, and the United States. However, since the research was initiated during the year of COVID-19 pandemic, the research team encountered significant limitations in training the facilitators to conduct the study and in establishing and monitoring data collection protocols, particularly through interviews conducted virtually or remotely across the regions. Compounding these obstacles was the sensitive nature of the subject matter, the need for effective communication channels to engage study participants, and the logistical complexities inherent in conducting online interviews in geographies like Cameroon, Egypt, and Uganda. Data collection efforts were initiated in Cameroon, Egypt, and Uganda. However, providing adequate data compensation to study participants proved challenging given the substantial time investment required for interviews, ranging from 60 to 90 minutes. Identifying and recruiting participants through appropriate communication channels was also a challenge. Consequently, research was abandoned in these three countries.

This book presents studies undertaken in India, Nigeria, Mexico, and the USA. In these studies, several challenges were also faced in data collection. These were due to mistrust and misunderstanding of the participants, who feared disclosing their personal information. There were differences in the language and perspectives of the participants and the researchers. Therefore, maintaining the integrity of the data was a challenge. Some participants hesitated to consent to audiotape because they were concerned about the invasion of privacy and how the recordings might be used. They were concerned that the researchers may take advantage of them and have hidden motives. There was also difficulty in determining and capturing real-time information as participants had difficulty remembering past events. Finally, analyzing large volumes of qualitative data to assess the information on self-care practices was very time-consuming.

To address the challenges outlined above for research undertaken in Mexico, India, Nigeria, and the United States, several strategies were implemented to expedite data collection and ensure comprehensive responses for high-quality data through continuous data monitoring. To achieve this, extensive orientation meetings and online workshops were organized for facilitators during the preparatory phase of the study. When interviews were conducted online, audio recordings were captured using a dedicated Zoom account with cloud storage accessible solely to the research team. Additionally, to adhere to the COVID-19 pandemic guidelines, in-person interviews were conducted with utmost care and precaution.

Interview guides were used to examine self-care practices adopted by the participants. Data was obtained on their lifestyle and interventions they used to promote sexual and reproductive health, such as condoms, gels, antibiotics, HIV testing kits, and others. Information was obtained on mental health problems and violence perpetrated by family members, partners, and the community. This research provided an understanding of participants' views about their self-care practices, how they obtained information on self-care interventions, and their motivations to use them. Information was also obtained on the barriers they faced and what they did if self-care practices failed.

Before initiating the study, participants were given consent forms that described the study. Their consent was taken, and confidentiality was assured. The interviews were recorded, transcribed, and checked for accuracy. The interview notes were sent to the interviewees for re-checking and validation.

To analyze the data collected, the researchers gathered all the transcripts, documents, and all other information. To familiarize themselves with the data, the researchers read the transcripts several times to make sense of them. After that, the points that help connect and categorize data were highlighted, and notes were made on the highlighted points. The data was coded by combining recurring themes such as language, opinions, and beliefs of the participants about their self-care practices related to sexual and reproductive health. Triangulation of data generated by key informant interviews (KIIs), in-depth interviews (IDIs), and focus group discussions (FGDs) made it possible to obtain comprehensive, reliable information on the complex and sensitive issues that were explored.

Relevance and importance of the study

This book focuses on self-care for promoting sexual and reproductive health and rights in young people, including high school students and college graduates (married and unmarried) in Mexico, India, Nigeria, and the USA. The study undertaken in Nigeria has been published in 2023 (5). The results of studies undertaken in Mexico, India, Nigeria, and the USA are reported in chapters two, three, and four of this book. Chapter five provides a comparative analysis of the results of the studies in all four countries. It discusses how different factors influenced the same age groups of young populations from different countries. Young people had varying levels of knowledge and undertook different self-care practices and attitudes towards self-care.

Since about 50 percent of the world's population does not have access to formal health services, it is crucial to implement self-care services to achieve Universal Health Coverage. The growth of the internet and m-health have greatly enhanced access to self-care interventions, especially for sexual and reproductive health and HIV prevention. This book addresses several important questions on self-care for SRHR of young people. These include the definition and scope of self-care. Why is self-care gaining importance? What populations should be prioritized for self-care for sexual and reproductive health and rights? What are important self-care SRHR interventions? Why do individuals choose self-care interventions? What is the role of self-care in preventing COVID-19? What research has been undertaken on self-care? What have we learned? And finally, how can the agenda be moved forward for promoting self-care to enhance sexual and reproductive health and rights? Answers to these questions are urgently needed for improving the SRHR of young people globally. This book will be important to a global audience of policy-makers, program implementers, academics, researchers, donors, and others.

References

1. World Health Organization. WHO guideline on self-care interventions for health and well-being revision. World Health Organization. 2022 Jun 27. https://www.who.int/publications/i/item/9789240052192

2. World Health Organization. Ethical, legal, human rights and social accountability implications of self-care interventions for sexual and reproductive health. World Health Organization Brocher Foundation, Hermance, Switzerland; 2018 Aug 16. https://www.who.int/publications/i/item/WHO-FWC-18.30

3. World Health Organization. WHO Guideline Recommendations on Digital Interventions for Health System Strengthening. World Health Organization Geneva. 2019. https://www.ncbi.nlm.nih.gov/books/NBK541902/

4. Pachauri S, Pachauri A & Mittal K. Sexual and reproductive health and

rights in India: Self-care for universal health coverage. Springer. 2022. https://link.springer.com/book/10.1007/978-981-16-4578-5

5. Pachauri S, Pachauri A, Mittal K, Pathak D & Philo Magdalene A. Gender dimensions of self-care for sexual and reproductive health and rights in Nigeria. In: Pachauri S, Verma RK, editors. Transforming unequal gender relations in India and beyond: An intersectional perspective on challenges and opportunities. Singapore: Springer Nature; 2023 p. 259–70. https://doi.org/10.1007/978-981-99-4086-8_16

Self-Care Experiences of High School and College Graduates in Mexico

Saroj Pachauri, Public Health Specialist, Trustee, Center for Human Progress, New Delhi, India, and Director, POP (Protect Our Planet) Movement, New York, USA

Ash Pachauri, Director, Center for Human Progress, New Delhi, India, and Senior Mentor, POP (Protect Our Planet) Movement, New York, USA

Norma Munoz Sevilla Patricia, Professor and Researcher, Centro Interdisciplinario de Investigaciones y Estudios Sobre Medio Ambiente y Desarrollo (CIIEMAD), Instituto Politécnico Nacional (IPN), Mexico, and Honorary Distinguished Mentor, POP (Protect Our Planet) Movement, New York, USA

Drishya Pathak, Research Associate, Center for Human Progress, New Delhi, India, and Global Youth Mentor, POP (Protect Our Planet) Movement, New York, USA

Komal Mittal, Research Associate, Center for Human Progress, New Delhi, India, and Global Youth Mentor, POP (Protect Our Planet) Movement, New York, USA

Philo Magdalene Antony Samy, Communications and Research Assistant, Center for Human Progress, New Delhi, India, and Global Youth Mentor, POP (Protect Our Planet) Movement, New York, USA

Nahid Perez Ayala, Youth Mentor, POP (Protect Our Planet) Movement, New York, USA

Abstract

Self-care is among the most promising approaches for achieving Universal Health Coverage. The growth and improved access to mobile technologies have paved the way for self-care to play a prominent role in improving the quality of sexual and reproductive health services in mid-level countries like Mexico. In this chapter, the authors focus on the knowledge, attitudes, and practices surrounding self-care interventions for sexual and reproductive health and rights. Qualitative research was undertaken in Mexico on high school students and college graduates (married and unmarried) to study their motivations for using self-care and their attitudes, practices, and experiences with self-care. The authors analyze their attitudes, practices, and experiences with self-care interventions such as contraceptives and self-injectables for family planning, self-medication for abortion, self-testing for pregnancy, and self-sampling for sexually transmitted infections (STIs). Challenges for self-care interventions encountered during the COVID-19 pandemic and factors responsible for adopting self-care interventions are also discussed. In addition, the relationship between gender and self-care interventions for sexual and reproductive health is examined. The authors conclude that self-care interventions must be systematically implemented to promote sexual and reproductive health and the rights of young people.

Background

"At least 400 million people worldwide lack access to the most essential health services. By 2035, there will be an estimated shortage of nearly 13 million healthcare workers." – World Health Organization (1)

Among the most promising and exciting new approaches to achieve the Universal Health Coverage (UHC) goals are self-care interventions. Quality self-care interventions have the potential to provide individuals with opportunities to make informed and timely decisions about their health and improve their choices to avail healthcare that is appropriate, accessible, and affordable.

With the increased availability and reliance on digital technologies, self-care is becoming an essential element for the achievement of UHC. The ultimate objective is to leave no one behind by ensuring access to preventive, promotive, and palliative healthcare for all. As the COVID-19 pandemic wreaked havoc globally, people were compelled to pay closer attention to their health and to adopt new behaviors to reduce the risk of transmission of infection. Self-care is now universally recognized as an essential means for preventing the spread of infection.

The World Health Organization (WHO) refers to self-care as patient-initiated interventions. Self-care enables people to take charge of their own health to prevent disease, limit illness, and promote and restore health. Self-care embraces the ability of people, including families and communities, in promoting health, preventing disease, maintaining health, and coping with illness and disability with or without the support of a healthcare provider (2). The overarching goal is to stimulate the systematic exchange of knowledge and ideas regarding the adoption and strategic implementation of self-care interventions for health and strengthen the role of multiple stakeholders, including non-governmental and community-based organizations, and members of vulnerable communities who played a significant role in its implementation, adoption, and dissemination.

In 2019, WHO launched the first consolidated guideline on self-care interventions for sexual and reproductive health and rights (SRHR) with the aim of defining the path to universal health coverage, leaving no one behind (3).

"While self-care is important in all aspects of health, it is particularly important – and particularly challenging to manage – for populations negatively affected by gender, political, cultural and power dynamics, and for vulnerable persons (e.g., people with disabilities and mental impairment). This is also true for self-care interventions for SRHR since many people are unable to exercise autonomy over

their bodies and are unable to make decisions around sexuality and reproduction." The WHO Consolidated Guideline on Self-care Interventions for Health: Sexual and Reproductive Health and Rights (3)

Since health autonomy and decision-making are the fundamental pillars that facilitate self-care interventions, there is a need to focus on the different dimensions of gender norms that influence self-care for SRHR. Inequitable gender norms have a negative impact on health outcomes. Challenges in decision-making, lack of autonomy, and inadequate access to information severely impact the use of self-care interventions. Therefore, equitable gender norms and consequent empowerment play a key role in promoting access to self-care interventions and improving sexual and reproductive health outcomes.

In this chapter, a study undertaken in Mexico to examine self-care interventions is presented. According to WHO's 2021 infographic snapshot on Mexico for sexual and reproductive health and rights, only 31.3 percent of adolescent girls (ages 15-24) have correct knowledge of HIV prevention. No data exists on implementing the Comprehensive Sexuality Education (CSE) Policy in primary and secondary schools (4). In Mexico, 79.8 percent of women who wanted contraception were satisfied with the modern method of contraception that they received, which included injections (5.3%), pills (3.6%), male condoms (10.9%), IUDs (16.3%) implants (6.3%), female sterilization (53.2%), and other modern methods (4.4%) (4). This report showed that while Mexico, as a lower-middle-income country, had many successes with regard to its national SRHR situation, there were several gaps in the program that still needed improvement, including strengthening of health systems, service delivery, and community engagement (4). In this chapter, self-care attitudes, practices, and experiences of high school students and college graduates (married and unmarried) in Mexico for promoting sexual and reproductive health and rights are examined.

The study in Mexico is a part of a multicountry study undertaken in India,

Mexico, USA, and Nigeria. Qualitative research was conducted with young people 14 to 28 years of age. Specific target groups were high school students and college graduates (married and unmarried). This chapter examines how aware young people are of sexual and reproductive health and how important it is for them to practice self-care. Their level of knowledge and awareness of various self-care interventions was assessed. How proactive are young people in terms of taking action for self-care as individuals? How does sexual behavior vary among different age groups? How is sexual behavior among young people impacted because of past relationships? What is the most reliable source of information for self-care interventions among young people? What are the various motivating and demotivating factors for practicing self-care? What is the role of gender and culture in practicing self-care for sexual and reproductive health? What factors lead to unfavorable conditions such as unwanted pregnancies and abortions and stigma against self-care practices? What factors affect motivation for using self-care products? And finally, what challenges related to self-care emerged during the COVID-19 pandemic?

Methodology

A qualitative research study designed to address the above objectives was undertaken in Quintana Roo, Jalisco, Tamaulipas, Durango, and Mexico State. Qualitative research methods allow greater spontaneity and interaction with research participants. They allow the participants to respond elaborately and in greater detail, giving a more nuanced understanding of the issues.

For this qualitative study, data was collected online and offline by conducting in-depth interviews (IDIs) and focus group discussions (FGDs) with high school students and college graduates (married and unmarried). The questionnaires aligned with the Self-care Values and Preferences Survey administered globally (4). However, additional components on gender norms, mental health, and COVID-19 were included in this study.

The interviews were conducted using interview guides. The interviews, approximately 90-120 minutes in length, were recorded. The recordings were transcribed and checked for accuracy. Eight IDIs and two FGDs were conducted with high school students. One of the participants was bisexual, and another was homosexual. Eight IDIs and two FGDs were conducted with college graduates. Of these, three were bisexuals, and three were married or were soon to be married.

The Institutional Review Board of Sigma (Sigma-IRB), Sigma Research and Consulting, New Delhi granted ethical approval for undertaking the study. Before conducting the research interviews, the interviewers described the objectives and importance of the study to all research participants. Participants were given consent forms that described the study risks and potential harm and ethics of informed consent and confidentiality. They were assured that the study posed minimal or no quantifiable harm to their physical or mental wellbeing. They were also told they could skip any questions they did not wish to answer and withdraw consent at any point during the interview, after which the data would be destroyed. Written and verbal consent was obtained from all participants. Confidentiality of the study participants was assured. The questionnaires were translated into Spanish to suit the language preference of the target population.

Transcripts were thoroughly read, and some unique similarities and differences were identified in the data collected. Based on this, several themes were used as probes for analysis. The themes included service provision, knowledge and behavior, male involvement, condom use, social support networks, sexually transmitted infections (STIs), including HIV, and pregnancy and childbirth.

Quotes were generously used to amplify the voices of the research participants and highlight the research results.

Self-care for sexual and reproductive health in Mexico: A literature review

Adolescent sexual and reproductive health (SRH) continues to pose a formidable challenge globally despite the efforts of governments in nations with varying income levels (5). There are various indicator categories for measuring adolescent SRH. These include violence (sexual abuse, intimate partner violence), reproductive health (adolescent fertility rate (AFR), abortion rate, maternal mortality ratio (MMR), knowledge of and attitudes towards menstrual hygiene, demand for family planning, antenatal care, postnatal care, and condom use) demographics, nutrition (prevalence of anemia, underweight, and obesity), mental health (prevalence rate and suicide rate), infectious/communicable diseases (HIV/STIs) parental connection and regulation, and other behavioral indicators (6). All of these factors influence the uptake of self-care interventions. High numbers within these categories, for example, 111 million cases of sexually transmitted infections (STIs) and 15 percent of new adult HIV cases among adolescents, are of global concern. And factors such as adolescent pregnancy, as defined by indicators such as AFR, are of serious concern (7). In this regard, self-care interventions can be considered a key pathway in addressing these concerns directly and indirectly.

The adolescent fertility rate (AFR), one of the reproductive health indicators, is the annual number of births to women aged 15-19 years per 1,000 women in that age group. According to World Data published in 2015, the AFR was recorded at 44 births per 1,000 adolescent women, with much higher rates in low-income countries (97 per 1,000) compared to middle-income countries (41 per 1,000) and high-income countries (19 per 1,000) (8). Although AFR has shown a considerable decrease in middle-income countries from 68 births per 1,000 adolescent women in 1990 to 37 births per 1,000 adolescent women in 2020, overall adolescent reproductive health remains a major concern, including in Mexico (9). In Mexico, which is a middle-income country, approximately 25.5 percent of male adolescents and 20.5 percent of female adolescents are sexually active. Yet, the use of self-care interventions like contraceptives is uncommon among them (10). Additionally, a quarter of women in Mexico say they have unmet contraceptive needs, which raises concerns about both the access to and attitude towards self-care practices (11)(12). There are other troubling aspects, including a lack of knowledge about how to seek help, low levels of prenatal care despite a high AFR, and a high rate of clandestine abortions (13).

Since 2007, the AFR has been 65.8 births per 1,000 adolescent women. Expectant mothers who were younger than 15 years of age had four times higher maternal mortality than older women, as per the 2009 Organization for Economic Co-operation and Development (OECD) data. Mexico, with the highest AFR, recorded about 76.4 births per 1,000 women aged 15–19 years in 2011, which declined to 70.5 births per 1,000 women in 2018 but is still very high (14). Approximately two out of every ten mothers who gave birth in Mexico in 2017 were under 20 (13). Factors affecting maternal mortality were anemia, hypertension, and premature birth (15). Since then, considerable progress has been made, and the AFR was 58 births per 1,000 adolescent women, according to the 2020 World Bank data (16). Several risk factors associated with a high rate of AFR and high mortality include individual, family, and social situations, low self-esteem, drug use, having a teenage mother and/or an absent father, not using family planning methods, and a lack of knowledge about sex. A number of these factors are expressions of inequality.

In Mexico, documented data shows that reproductive health outcomes are mainly related to inequalities in access to health services, which are differentiated by socioeconomic strata. For example, the rate of pregnancies in adolescents ranges from 97 per 1,000 pregnancies in the poorest groups to 15 per 1,000 pregnancies in the most affluent classes (13). As multi-level barriers to health systems and services remain a major concern, knowledge and practice of self-care interventions can be of great significance in addressing some of these gaps. Data from a study in 2015 published in the State of the World's Mothers annual report showed that the contraceptive use prevalence for the southernmost Mexican states, such as Chiapas, was 35.5 percent, and for the rest of the country, it was 59.9 percent (13). As per the National Population Council, all these risk factors were further exacerbated by COVID-19 with an estimated 30 percent increase in unwanted pregnancies (12). Thus, AFR and unwanted pregnancy are major public health issues in Mexico as well as in much of Latin America. In view of this, as a preventive and self-empowering strategy, adequate knowledge and literacy surrounding self-care interventions for SRH would be a step in the right direction.

Addressing unintended pregnancy and abortion concerns

As adolescents have higher levels of unintended pregnancies, they face a higher risk of abortion. Adolescents are disproportionately affected by unwanted pregnancies, which give rise to a range of additional health problems. Data indicates that approximately two million adolescents access abortion services annually, often under risky and illegal conditions. About 60 percent of unwanted pregnancies occur in this population globally, resulting in adolescent mortality (17). In Latin America, maternal mortality among adolescents is a major concern. It is primarily caused by unsafe abortions, with an increased risk of complications arising from delayed access to abortion services (18).

In response to the persistent trend of AFR and the high incidence of first-birth abortions, Mexico City and some other states decriminalized first trimester abortion in 2007 and promptly integrated these services into public sector programs. While adolescents were eligible for abortion services, those under the age of 18 required adult consent. Despite these efforts, the law remains highly restrictive in Mexico with limited legal exceptions such as rape, risk to health or life, and was not consistently applied across the 31 states outside of Mexico City until 2021 (14). In 2021, the Supreme Court of Mexico decriminalized abortion, ruling that the constitution prohibits the criminalization of the procedure. Since then, nine states have legalized abortion, and four states allow abortion for any reason during the first trimester (12).

In Mexico, a key self-care practice is medical abortion, which includes using a combination of two drugs, mifepristone and misoprostol. However, in accordance with the WHO guidelines, women who are unable to obtain a legal abortion in their state or prefer to handle it privately often opt for medical abortion at home using misoprostol alone (19). Misoprostol is available over the counter in every state to treat ulcers. This makes it easier to get an abortion with it alone rather than with a combination of drugs, although both are equally safe. Abortion services are also offered at private sector facilities. However, these facilities are not obligated to report data which results in a significant limitation of available data, particularly for women under the age of 25.

According to a study conducted by Darney et al., in which clinical data on abortion from the Interrupción Legal de Embarazo abortion program in Mexico City between 2007 and 2016 was assessed while considering various socio-demographic factors, it was found that 41 percent of the abortions were performed in women seeking to prevent their first birth. These nulliparous women were educated; 46 percent had a high school education, while 29 percent were from universities. Out of the 41 percent, 17 percent were aged 12-17 years and 64 percent were 18-24 years of age. This study also analyzed the rate of first birth abortions among students and unemployed women under the age groups of 12-17 and 18-24 years. Students and employed women had a 90 percent probability of using abortion to prevent their first birth, which was higher as compared to women who did not work outside the home (14). However, this study was conducted only in Mexico City and only on those women who registered themselves under the scheme. Consequently, data for illegal and unsafe abortion complications among other adolescent groups was missing. Adolescent pregnancies can heighten the risk of poverty due to girls dropping out of school, which negatively impacts their physical and personal development (12). This chain of negative consequences can be minimized with the appropriate facilitation of self-care interventions for prevention and promotion.

Another study conducted in 2014 by Andrea et al., where the authors compared the MMR in adolescents and women in other age groups across 144 countries, found that in the five-year periods between 2000 and 2004 and between 2005 and 2009, the MMR had declined from 43 to 36 for the age group of 15-19 years and from 43 to 35 for the 20-24 years age group (20). However, overall, findings revealed that 10 percent of maternal deaths each year occurred in adolescents aged 15-19 in the 144 countries studied. Due to a lack of data from Mexico and because of unreported cases, there was a high level of uncertainty in the results (20). It is, however, well known that such data for adolescent girls is limited.

Improving access to sexual and reproductive health services

The main drivers of illness among youth are risky sexual behaviors due to low levels of awareness and inadequate access to contraception, leading to a significant impact on morbidity (21). There is inadequate knowledge, low access, and low practice of self-care interventions. It is, therefore, imperative that adolescents have access to safe and effective contraception in order to limit child mortality, improve maternal health, and address critical public health concerns posed by HIV/AIDS, as specified in the United Nations Millennium Development Goals (22).

The provision of sexual reproductive health and rights (SRHR) services continues to be a challenge for adolescents and young people (AYP), particularly those residing in low- and middle-income countries (LMICs). Despite enormous progress in public health including in the area of self-care interventions, adolescents still lack access to basic healthcare services (23). This disparity was highlighted in the 2018 Guttmacher-Lancet Commission report, which showed that more than 200 million women were unable to obtain modern contraceptives, and more than 350 million unsafe abortions took place worldwide (24). In 2020, there were reportedly 777,000 births among adolescents under 15 years of age, with a majority of these occurring in Africa (58%), followed by Asia (28%), and Latin America and the Caribbean (14%) (24). By the time they turned 19, almost half the adolescents from developing countries were sexually active, partly due to early marriage, and half of them had experienced unplanned pregnancies (25). Additionally, it is worth mentioning that adolescents and women in general are more susceptible to sexually transmitted infections (STIs), including HIV (26). In this context of high-risk associated with adolescents from LMICs, self-care interventions are an important means for promoting adolescent sexual and reproductive health.

Latin America is home to a majority of HIV positive people (45%) with adolescents and young people making up a sizable portion of the population (27). Since adolescents tend to be impulsive and often fantasize, they are more prone to have incorrect ideas about sexuality and are unable to assess the risks associated with sex. As a result, they fail to think through the implications of their actions and delay seeking medical care. Given the rising incidence of sexually transmitted infections in low- and middle- income countries despite widely established prevention programs, the issue of adolescent sexual health has become a matter of significant concern in these regions (28). Studies show that adolescents who engage in sexual activity early on and those who believe that they are too young to fall ill or die are more vulnerable to contracting STIs. Age is widely acknowledged as a key determinant in the practice of risk behaviors. Numerous authors concur that early initiation of sexual activity increases the risk of both unwanted pregnancies and STIs. This is due to the fact that the adolescent brain is still undergoing a process of cognitive development and adolescents are reconstructing their thoughts, beliefs, and personalities that govern their sexual conduct (29). With these factors at play, literacy regarding self-care interventions for SRHR should be prioritized in dealing with adolescents' risky behaviors.

Latin America is improving in the provision of services, including self-care interventions targeted at key populations for the prevention and treatment of HIV and other sexually transmitted infections. Sex education is crucial for preventing unintended pregnancy among young people and combating sexual violence and abuse. Providing knowledge about reproductive health, the menstrual cycle, and contraception empowers girls to make informed decisions and practice self-care. When adolescents and youth are informed, they are better equipped to reject sexual abuse and report such occurrences. They are also able to delay sexual activity until they are ready (12). Promoting sex education is a global challenge that must be addressed. Latin America, especially Mexico, has made significant progress in promoting sexual and reproductive health and gender equality. Mexico's Constitution (Article 3) mandates that schools provide educational material to promote gender sensitivity and provide information on sexuality and reproductive health (12).

Sexually transmitted infections (STIs) and maternal mortality and morbidity are major global public health concerns in adolescents (30)(31). Teen pregnancy can have significant negative effects on maternal and child health and can exacerbate gender and social disparities (30).

Education is a major factor that promotes self-care in the uptake of contraception and prevents pregnancy. For example, a report issued in Mexico in 2001 indicated that only 48 percent of illiterate women in stable relationships were using some contraceptive method, in contrast to 75 percent of women who had completed at least 9 years of schooling (4)(32).

The recent analysis of Demographic and Health Surveys (DHS) on young single women (15 to 24 years old) across eight Latin American countries (Bolivia, Brazil, Colombia, Dominican Republic, Guatemala, Nicaragua, Paraguay, and Peru) confirmed that there was an increase in the trend of premarital sexual activity in the region. The study also found an increase in the uptake of contraception, particularly condoms. This data indicates a correlation between contraceptive protection and conception rates. However, the authors concluded that an increase in the uptake of contraception was not adequate to offset the increased risk of pregnancy-related to increased sexual activity (18).

There is a dearth of easily accessible data pertaining to the sexual and reproductive health of young people and self-care interventions in the Latin American region. Available information reveals broad patterns, including a rise in premarital sexual activity, an increase in the incidence of HIV among younger demographic groups, and persistent or increasing adolescent fertility rates with high rates of unintended pregnancy and risky abortion procedures. Furthermore, the data implies that sexual coercion may be an issue for young people across the region (18).

Despite the clear need for improved reproductive healthcare, no comprehensive evaluation of the quality of such interventions for adolescents has been undertaken to date. The impact of a school-based HIV prevention program on Mexican secondary school students was studied by the Mexican Institute of Family and Population Research (IMIFAP), the Mexican Ministry of Public Education (SEP), and the Horizons Program. In Mexico, all public schools must implement sexuality education and teacher training programs, although the specific content is left to the discretion of individual states. These programs are considered a formal part of the curriculum, and students must pass these subjects as they would in any other course (33). An assessment of the quality of sexual and reproductive healthcare is crucial in addressing barriers and problems in the delivery of care for promoting self-care interventions among adolescents.

Uptake of contraceptives and lubricants

Globally, the self-care practice of contraception to control fertility has been recognized. Studies show that there is an association between education and increased knowledge and use of contraceptives (18). Unmet need for contraception is an effective indicator of the gap between reproductive desire and the accessibility of contraception (34). The proportion of fertile individuals who do not use contraceptives while intending to space or limit their childbearing is known as the unmet need for contraception (Potts et al. 2009) (35). Despite successful programs to promote family planning, unmet need has been an ongoing challenge in Mexico, particularly for young people and those living in rural areas. Approximately 10 percent of the country's needs are unmet, rising to 26 percent among women aged 15-19 (35). Unintended pregnancy, which encompasses pregnancies that are either unexpected (earlier or later than desired) or undesired, is the result of contraceptive unmet needs, contraceptive failure, or improper use of contraceptives.

Research shows that there are fewer unwanted pregnancies when free contraception is widely available and comprehensive sex education is pro-vided (Gold 2006; Darroch 2001). In accordance with established formal policy, the Mexican government offers services and education to promote self-care, i.e., provides access to contraceptives to reduce unmet needs, and thereby decreases unplanned pregnancies. State health officials state that government initiatives have lowered the incidence of adverse health consequences, including adolescent pregnancy (35).

Factoring in mental health

The general population has been shown to experience increased psychological distress and uncertainty during public health emergencies (36). Economically disadvantaged people and those with chronic diseases are most vulnerable to developing mental health problems, especially during pandemics such as COVID-19, as are women, older persons, migrant workers, health personnel, and students (37).

After the first cases of SARS-CoV-2 virus infection were reported at the end of February 2020, Mexico has reported significant death and case fatality rates due to COVID-19. Restricted movements during the lockdown had an imminent and immediate impact on students' lifestyles and caused a number of psychological problems, such as stress, anxiety, and depression (38).

People who were in seclusion due to quarantine experienced frustration and boredom. They worried about getting the infection and were concerned for family and friends. Thus, their emotional wellbeing was compromised (39). Adults face psychological consequences such as boredom, fear of infection, dissatisfaction, frustration, and financial issues. COVID-19 also increased the risk of mental health problems in the general population (40)(41)(42).

At the onset of the pandemic, the Mexican government encouraged preventive health practices, including keeping a physical distance, using hand sanitizers, and staying at home. Public health actions such as closing down mass gathering places like churches, schools, and shopping centers were enforced. These public health actions significantly impacted the economy (43)(42). On March 23, 2020, the COVID-19 outbreak in Mexico resulted in school closures. Schools in Mexico did not reopen until May 2021, when the immunization campaigns were rolled out among teachers (44). Latin America experienced the highest number of school closures worldwide during the pandemic, with an average closure duration of 217 days. In comparison, the length of closures was limited in the Middle East and North Africa (167 days), Sub-Saharan Africa (116 days), Asia (107 days), Europe (93 days), and the U.S. and Canada (46 days). Prior to May 2021, when schools began operating again, Mexico ranked eighth among countries with the most days of school closure (45)(46).

Worldwide, adolescent girls die from maternal health problems more frequently than adult women (8). The pandemic increased the rate of depression in medical students, with women experiencing more severe problems, according to a study by Gonzalez et al. published in 2022. Females and young people were more prone to be affected by anxiety, depression, stress, and distress (42). Students receiving psychiatric treatment had a rise in the rates of depression. However, the fact that they were receiving treatment acted as a mitigating factor for the rise in depression rates (47).

Similar findings were observed in Turkey, Brazil, Peru, and China (48)(49)(50)(51). It has been hypothesized that women are more likely than men to experience stress and anxiety disorders, which can affect their development and can aggravate other conditions such as eating disorders and post-traumatic stress disorders (PTSD) (52)(53). With reference to age, Mexicans under 40 years of age were more likely to get mental health conditions. For instance, Ahmed et al. showed that young people (aged 21–40 years) were more susceptible to mental health problems and alcohol consumption (54). According to Glowacz et al. people between 18 and 30 years of age had lower levels of occupational activity, fewer social interactions, poorer living conditions, and higher levels of anxiety, despair, and ambiguity than older adults (55)(42). Maintaining good mental health is a crucial and important issue for COVID-19. Research is required to determine how mental health problems and the number of suicides related to COVID-19 can be decreased.

Mental health in the post-COVID-19 era should not be ignored. Mental health problems were common in Mexico, and the primary risk factors associated with them were anxiety, depression, stress, and distress. The availability of this information should make it possible to develop programs tailored to the needs of the population to reduce the adverse impact of the pandemic by: (1) promoting mental wellness and reducing distress, (2) establishing primary screening services for mental health, and (3) integrating basic mental health services within primary care for early detection. Evidence-based prevention and treatment strategies should be designed and implemented to reduce the adverse psychological impact of the COVID-19 pandemic (42).

Factoring in gender disparities

The COVID-19 pandemic affected more women than men in Mexico's workforce. Beyond the significant drop in labor force participation, the pandemic had an impact on a number of areas of gender parity. Women bore the brunt of the increased domestic burden caused by the pandemic, especially child care and education. This, coupled with the demands of telecommuting, meant that the rates of exhaustion and anxiety were also higher in women than in men.

Between the first quarter of 2020 and the same period in 2021, 1.7 million people in Mexico left the labor market; of those 84 percent were women. Men's labor force participation increased twice as quickly as women's after the recession. In addition, a higher proportion of women than men considered slowing down their careers or giving up paid work altogether due to its effects on their mental health. The group most impacted was women who had children. Ninety percent of the women who left their jobs during the first year of the pandemic had children. Women's professions were more negatively impacted than men's because of their increased household burden and higher levels of stress (56). Access to health services, including SRHR, was affected by gender as well as by sociocultural and economic factors.

Existing gender disparities as well as sociocultural and economic divides were worse in women as a result of the COVID-19 pandemic's disruptions of standard health services including community level platforms where AYP receive information and support for SRHR services. Adolescents and young women were expected to bear the brunt because of existing gender inequalities (26).

COVID-19: A new factor for SRHR

UNESCO reported that more than 861.7 million children and youth in 107 countries were affected by nationwide school closures, travel restrictions that impeded economic and social transactions, and existing inequalities. It is important to document how the pandemic affected AYP's access to SRHR services (26).

The COVID-19 pandemic severely damaged health infrastructure worldwide, ranging from human resources to medicines and other supplies to providing psychosocial support to those who were infected with the virus. Because of COVID-19, several healthcare providers had either died or had been infected.

Access to information by AYP was further restricted because of travel and social distancing restrictions. A UNFPA global poll conducted in 2021 found that mothers were reluctant to discuss SRHR with their adolescent daughters (57). SRHR services continued to be difficult for priority groups such as AYP in the majority of LMICs due to weak health systems. The pandemic lowered the quality of life and basically impeded the achievement of important SRHR targets of the global Sustainable Development Goals (SDGs) for AYP. The health system needs to prioritize the provision of SRHR services. In this regard, self-care interventions can be significant for prioritizing SRHR for adolescents and young people (AYP).

Research results

Accessing information about sexual and reproductive health and rights

Our study showed that most high school students within the age group of 14 and 18 years were sexually active. In the focus group discussion with eight boys, only one was sexually inactive. Boys were generally uncomfortable talking about the changes in their bodies with anyone, especially with their parents. For the group of high school boys, the main source of information regarding sexual and reproductive health was school, and for some, it was the family or social campaigns. High school students were aware of different sexual practices, including oral, vaginal, and anal sex.

Students from public schools and Catholic schools in Mexico said that they were aware of sexual and reproductive health. This information was provided to them as part of the school curriculum. Only after joining college did they gain a better understanding of self-care products. Our study showed that young people's knowledge of contraceptive methods was limited to the use of condoms by males to prevent pregnancy and sexually transmitted infections while engaging in sexual activities. Female students were more aware and had a better understanding of self-care products for birth control and abortion management. Compared to boys, girls were more aware of the side effects of the contraceptives.

"Compared to other products, I feel condoms are much better as they are used externally."

A sexually active 24-year-old college graduate

"My source of knowledge is through school, campaigns, and my family. For me, it is being aware of what one does and being aware of using protection to take care of oneself and the other person and thus have good health."

A sexually active 18-year-old male

"Discussing sexual and reproductive health in the Mexican context is as important as discussing mental health problems. It is necessary to educate young people regarding reproduction. For me and my partner, sexual and reproductive health is very important. We do not want to get any sexually transmitted infections, and we also want to prevent pregnancy by using birth control methods."

A sexually active 18-year-old high school female student

The use of technology is very common among young people. With the easy availability and accessibility of information technology and their curiosity about accessing services, young participants were knowledgeable about the use of self-care interventions for SRHR. However, they were concerned about receiving misinformation. They preferred to receive accurate information from experts.

"I think I would look it up to make sure that if there are any menstrual irregularities, I look it up to ensure that everything is okay. If I have any doubts, I don't necessarily have to go to the gynecologist to resolve the problem."

An 18-year-old female student

Self-care interventions for sexual and reproductive health and rights

Perceptions of self-care

Self-care has a different meaning for everyone. Our study shows differences in the meaning of "self-care" among young people. For some, self-care meant preventing infection. For some, it meant trying to know themselves and their emotional needs. For some, it was related to awareness and self-respect. Some related self-care to mental health and providing basic needs such as proper food, clean water, a safe place, and an active lifestyle. However, the pandemic changed the meaning of self-care in everyone's lives. COVID-19 brought a clearer meaning and importance of self-care in everyone's life. It gave people a space to talk freely about their mental health conditions and added impetus for seeking information. It encouraged people to exercise to remain active and to follow a healthy lifestyle, including eating good food, exercising, practicing yoga, and following safety regulations set up by the government.

"It [promoting self-care] was really critical for emergency services because the healthcare system was overloaded. If people really know the color code, they can identify the codes and can get access to emergency services."

A sexually active 26-year-old homosexual male doctor

"So many people started to adopt self-care, which provided an opportunity to see it as an important part of life and something that can be done at home."

A sexually active 24-year-old homosexual female doctor

Knowledge and accessibility of self-care interventions

Information that high school had was limited to what was shared in the school or by the family. Half of them were not involved in sexual activities. They were also aware of auto-sexual practices. High school students were more comfortable looking at various self-care interventions online because they felt uncomfortable discussing them with their families or doctors. Some students mentioned that movies and social media were their sources of SRH information. They would go to a doctor if they could not get information online or from their friends.

"I look on the internet because I think I can find that information on my own and save myself a visit to the doctor. I will probably feel uncomfortable talking about this with a doctor."

An 18-year-old sexually inactive female

"In Mexico, it is very common for young girls (12–15 years) to have premature pregnancies. So, sexual campaigns have been undertaken in elementary schools. This subject is discussed in government schools, and it may be taboo within families. Religious traditions also make it difficult to discuss this."

A sexually active 25-year-old married female

"Movies and the internet have usually been the source of my information."

A sexually active 22-year-old bisexual female

Our study shows that college graduates were more aware of sexual and reproductive health than high school students. They also had more proactive attitudes. High school girls were more proactive in getting diagnosed if they had symptoms related to sexual and reproductive health as compared to high school boys. The study showed that sexually active boys from high schools commonly used lubricants during sexual intercourse. Study participants also reflected on the importance of partners' consent before making SRH decisions. One of the participants mentioned, *"I know about SRH. However, I'm not very experienced. I follow some blogs on sexual and reproductive health. My fiance talked about it. We have mutual consent about our sexual relationship."*

"At the beginning of the pandemic, I had a little secretion in one of my breasts. I visited a doctor and got the blot test done for prolactin."

A sexually active 22-year-old unmarried bisexual female

"I know about pills, patches, condoms, IUDs, vasectomy, and tubal ligation. I started in elementary school, where they would give talks about it. But as I got older, I had access to information through social media and conversations with friends."

An 18-year-old girl

Over-the-counter contraceptives

All study participants, especially college graduates who were currently in relationships or had been in the past, knew about self-care interventions and protective methods. And most of them used contraceptive methods, usually condoms. Young people were also aware of other birth control methods, but they had incomplete information about these methods. There was limited use of birth control pills due to the belief that they cause side-effects and hormonal imbalance.

High school students were aware of most of the contraceptive methods like hormonal implants, birth control pills, female condoms, abstinence, IUDs, over-the-counter emergency contraception, and patches. Similar to college graduates, male high school students were not well informed about the effects of hormonal contraception or the emergency pill. Four high school boys admitted that their female partners had used over-the-counter emergency contraception. This shows that there is risky sexual behavior among high school students. They were not even aware of self-administered contraception.

"Maybe not that much, but yeah, something about it. Safe sex– may be using protection– is what I think it means."

A sexually active 25-year-old male college student

"I am aware of condoms, contraceptive pills, hormonal implants, IUDs, vasectomy, and abstinence. I don't know the name, but keeping a count of the days of the woman's menstrual cycle is another method. I got this information in a biology

32

class and also from my parents."

A 17-year-old male student

"I haven't used any contraceptives. I am aware that we can get these from pharmacies or health centers. But I don't know the side-effects they will have."

A sexually active 18-year-old male student

Self-medication

College graduates argued that one should decide about one's own body. However, after-intervention support is lacking in Mexico. Knowledge about birth control exists among young high school boys who admit that there are many early pregnancies due to a lack of sexual education and that both boys and girls should be aware of birth control and should not resort to abortion. High school boys stated that they had been informed about the use of condoms when they were children. But what they lacked was a sense of responsibility, which led to abortion. Self-care interventions were known to most of the sexually active males. But how to procure self-medication for abortion was known to only a few. One high school student from the state of Quintana Roo, Mexico, mentioned that the abortion pill is available without any prescription at the pharmacy.

"There are many unwanted pregnancies due to lack of awareness and responsibility."

A sexually active 18-year-old from high school boy

Menstrual hygiene

Most of the girls were aware of menstrual hygiene. They received this information from their mothers and older sisters. Some high school students received information about menstruation through their school curriculum and campaigns on menstrual hygiene. Our study showed that boys were also aware of menstrual hygiene but were not comfortable discussing it.

Their knowledge was limited to the use of sanitary napkins by girls during menstruation.

Self-testing and self-monitoring

Awareness among college graduates about self-care testing kits was limited to the use of pregnancy test kits. Awareness about self-care interventions like HPV, HIV, and other STIs was generated through campaigns organized by universities.

The data showed that high school students had very little information about self-testing/sampling or self-monitoring methods for SRH and some very common sexually transmitted infections like HPV and others. Knowledge about HPV infections was almost negligible among high school students. College graduates were better informed.

"A papillomavirus test was done with the cells of the cervix. This was done through the campaign at the university. They also conducted the syphilis test with a drop of blood."

A sexually active 22-year-old bisexual female

Motivations for the uptake of self-care interventions and the associated stigma

Mexico, a country recognized as Catholic, has a high number of sexually active adolescents. However, when it comes to information and awareness of the subject of sexual and reproductive health, there is stigma, and there are cultural taboos. Self-care products such as contraceptives and self-sampling kits are available in the market and at pharmacies. But it is difficult to get them because of stigma, especially by women and girls. This stigma affects their attitudes and behaviors when accessing and using self-care products. Young people lack a safe space to access these products which puts many lives at risk.

"I think there are still many taboos, especially on the subject of sexual and reproductive health. Products are available in pharmacies. But they are not accessible because of stigma, especially for women. It is easier for a man to buy contraceptives than it is for a woman."

An 18-year-old high school girl

"I would ask my partner to buy over-the-counter hormonal contraception from the pharmacy but I would buy a pregnancy test-kit from the pharmacy myself."

An 18-year-old girl

Over-the-counter contraception

Our study shows that most males preferred to use condoms during sexual intercourse. Condoms are easily available and are pocket-friendly. Female condoms are not easily accessible and are available only at special pharmacies. Male condoms were preferred. Most of the participants were not aware of the vaginal ring and its usage. But the medical students who were interviewed mentioned its long-lasting benefits and said that it is important to maintain proper hygiene while using a vaginal ring which is a demotivating factor for using it.

"Female condoms are hard to find and are only available at special pharmacies."

A sexually active 22-year-old bisexual single female

It was not easy for young people to obtain over-the-counter hormonal contraception. High school students were not aware of these products. Most young people face the challenge of being judged by their peers. They were also worried about the side effects of hormonal contraceptives. A 20-year-old sexually active bisexual female discussed the stigma of using hormonal contraception.

"I would feel good using it, but I would feel judged by my family, and I am quite worried about the side-effects."

A sexually active 20-year-old bisexual unmarried female

Menstrual hygiene

Most mothers did not like their daughters to use tampons and menstrual cups due to cultural beliefs. Young high school girls and college graduates were more likely to use tampons and menstrual cups instead of using sanitary pads, as sanitary pads caused a lot of pollution and were not environmentally-friendly.

"I used to swim, and for that, I used tampons, which was a major problem for my mother. After turning 17, I started using menstrual cups secretly as my mother did not like it due to cultural beliefs. It is easier to find sanitary pads in the supermarket. However, menstrual cups and tampons are hard to find and are only available at pharmacies and online marketplaces."

A sexually active 22-year-old unmarried bisexual female

Self-sampling and self-management

Both high school students and college graduates had little knowledge about self-sampling. Most were not aware of the terminologies HPV, HIV, and STIs. Very few college graduates and married couples, especially medical professionals such as microbiologists, chemists, and physicians had this knowledge. Most college students obtained information through campaigns organized by universities on their campuses. School students had limited sexual and reproductive health information. Many said that there was stigma at healthcare facilities and hospitals for testing. Easy-to-access self-testing kits were in great demand. Research participants discussed the risk factors involved in self-sampling. Getting tested at a healthcare facility seemed like a better option to them. Most participants preferred to follow the protocol before getting tested.

"I do not want to go to a doctor if it is possible to self-test. One of my friends felt embarrassed when he had to get himself tested."

A sexually active 25-year-old unmarried male

"At this age, I would feel insecure if someone sees me and gossips."

An 18-year-old high school girl

Young people were not fully aware of the self-management of abortion. However, they emphasized that there was a stigma associated with using abortion pills among peers and in society in general. They were concerned about being judged by society and were not fully informed about the legality of abortion.

"I heard about abortion pills two months ago. But I do not know if it is legal or illegal. It is illegal in my state, but I think it should be made legal."

A sexually active 25-year-old unmarried male

"I would feel comfortable going to buy it if I didn't feel judged by my family. I do not think I would tell them."

A sexually active 20-year-old bisexual unmarried female

Young people, especially high school students, were not aware of the need for self- or home-monitoring during pregnancy. College graduates were aware to some extent. However, they never practiced it at home. On discussing self-care products, most were positive in supporting home monitoring during pregnancy since there were few healthcare facilities during the pandemic.

Hormone therapy for gender affirmation

Medical professionals who belonged to the queer community were aware of hormone therapy for gender affirmation. However, they did not have enough knowledge about the process of gender affirmation. They said that gender affirmation therapy is very expensive. The government should support those who would like to use it. They mentioned that it is important to consult a physician before planning for gender affirmation. They felt that counseling was also important for the process.

Self-care for sexual and reproductive health and rights through a gender lens

Our study showed that once boys attained puberty, they were asked to make lifestyle changes. Boys usually faced the pressure of getting jobs so they could take care of their families. It was clear that high school boys did not get any information from their parents to make lifestyle changes. All they were told was related to gaining maturity and responsibility. Most young people shared that the consent of both partners was important for engaging in sexual practices.

"Being an adult is being mature, more responsible, behaving as such, having job pressure and stress."

A sexually active 17-year-old boy

"With my ex-boyfriends, I had relations without condoms. I asked one of them to get the blood test."

A sexually active 22-year-old bisexual female

Males have very little knowledge about self-care interventions and little to absolutely no knowledge about abortion. Despite different knowledge levels, they were clear on the principle that both males and females should have equal responsibility while engaging in sex.

"I think it should be a task for both partners. They should take care of themselves. She should take birth control pills or hormones. It is not just a task of one person."

A 22-year-old college student

High school boys mentioned that their families did talk to them about SRH.

However, they did not feel comfortable discussing SRH with their parents. The average age of sexually active high school boys was 14-15 years. High school boys were allowed to go out alone and on trips, sometimes without permission. But when it came to making decisions related to their health, they relied on their parents.

"SRH is very important for me and for my partner. I got this information at school and from my peers. My family does not feel comfortable discussing SRH with me."
A 17-year-old high school boy

"No, I don't have enough information so I need to read because I am not aware of all the things that we can do."
A sexually active 25-year-old male

Women were more participatory, possibly due to the Latino culture, in which women show greater interest in caring for their health. On the other hand, family support is a protective factor against risky sexual behavior. In our study, we found that the majority of adolescents lived with their parents and were supported financially and emotionally by them.

"SRH was not important for my ex-boyfriend. For my girlfriends, it is very important. If something is important and should be practiced, my girlfriend will tell me."
A sexually active 22-year-old bisexual female

Older adolescents were more likely to practice risky sexual behaviors. This could be due to the fact that during adolescence, they are in a process of constant change, which makes them vulnerable and results in negative consequences for their health. They are also affected by peer pressure. Our study shows that adults began their first sexual relationship around the age of 15. This shows that they are more likely to practice risky sexual behaviors because they are in a stage of experimentation and discovery of their sexuality where the forbidden and mysterious are a constant challenge.

Due to a lack of correct information, it was found that boys indulged in more risky behaviors, and they started sexual activities at an earlier age as compared to girls of the same age. Older adolescents have a higher level of resilience. Boys had a high degree of resilience, which indicates that they have a greater capacity to address sexual risks.

Our study shows that in Mexico, young people across genders did not feel comfortable discussing birth control with their partners. They shared that they wanted to discuss it with their partners, friends, or the doctor. Discussing birth control and contraceptive use with mothers is still a taboo in Mexico, particularly among those in the lower socioeconomic strata. It was also observed that young people, especially adolescent girls, were more interested than adolescent boys in receiving correct information on sexual matters. Most high school boys in our study were sexually active but had little or no information.

"I am aware of birth control. I do not feel comfortable discussing it with my mother."

A sexually active 21-year-old female

In focus group discussions, high school students were aware of sexual assault and also aware of the early signs of sexual assault, like good touch and bad touch. In the group interview, the boys said that they had not experienced sexual abuse. Two girls had experienced sexual assault. One by her gynecologist. The other felt harassed when she went for her pregnancy test. She was treated unpleasantly at the healthcare facility. However, few or no statistics are available on such assault victims. It was also observed that girls who experienced sexual assault were not fully aware of whether or not to consider it as sexual assault.

Self-care and the COVID-19 factor

Study participants felt that they could obtain services from the healthcare system in Mexico during the pandemic. However, they mentioned that due to the fear of getting infected, they preferred self-care at home which avoided contact. In Mexico, health services were available. Medicines from pharmacies were only available with a prescription. Getting check-ups was possible with the limitation of commuting to places and waiting for long hours at the facility to get tested. Some participants mentioned that the use of contraceptives decreased during the pandemic due to travel restrictions because *"we were not able to meet our partners."*

"We haven't experienced any difference in the health system during the pandemic. Because of being afraid of getting infected, we prefer self-care."
A sexually active high school student

"The idea of getting sick was terrifying. Every hospital was a COVID hospital, and private clinics were very expensive. Pharmacies were not allowed to sell anything without a prescription."
A sexually active 22-year-old bisexual female

"We have lived it. Hospitals were overwhelmed. Once, I almost fainted because they kept me waiting. Facilities were in very bad condition as they lacked resources."
A sexually active 20-year-old bisexual female

Our study also showed that there was an increase in violence and sexual assault. The burden of responsibility fell on women as they were forced to leave their professions because of responsibilities at home. Most male participants shared responsibilities at home.

During the pandemic, our study participants suffered mental health problems with increased psychological disorders and stress. Those living alone or stuck in different cities at their campuses said they felt lonely and anxious. Being locked in one place without the family created a difficult situation for them. Some participants mentioned having issues in their relationships with their partners because they could not meet them, especially during the lockdown period.

"It was weird in the beginning as I could not see my family members. It was a little challenging. It was weird for us to get used to being together again. Not seeing my friends was really hard. Earlier, I used to go out to see my friends when I was in my hometown, but it was really weird to come back home to Guadalajara. I like being with my parents and my cats."

A sexually active 21-year-old female

"I faced issues with my boyfriend as it was hard for us to meet and see each other, and ultimately, we broke up."

A sexually active 21-year-old female

"All my family members were in different locations, which scared me. I was all alone in Mexico during that time. I was concerned about my health and kept myself busy doing other tasks."

A 27-year-old female

High school students discussed the issues of having classes online. Virtual school was challenging. Their education was affected. One of the participants mentioned *"it was hard and I [a 22-year-old bisexual female] faced anxiety. The classes were all online. Some of the professors communicated with us but some did not. I couldn't go out as I was at the computer constantly."*

Some of the study participants had mental health problems due to the pandemic situation. They had to take therapy to deal with their anxiety. Participants mentioned different reasons and situations that affected their mental health. The impact was longer than expected. A feeling of loss was a major issue that affected young people.

"I was pretty anxious, as if I was doing nothing. I am happy when I am out. Even though I am vaccinated, I feel anxious. I am back to school; I started taking therapy. In March, I lost a family member; I started to feel depressed and so got back to my

classes. I was not prepared. I started therapy to deal with the loss and anxiety."

A sexually active 22-year-old bisexual female

Discussion

Our study shows that young people had some understanding of self-care interventions for SRH, including contraceptive methods, self-testing kits for pregnancy, and, to an extent, self-sampling for STIs. They had received this information primarily from campaigns run at schools and universities, online platforms, and from their peers. It is important to note that while youth often accessed information from the internet, there was always the fear of misinformation.

Young people's knowledge was limited and incomplete. For example, they knew that condoms should be used to prevent pregnancy but were unaware that condoms can prevent STIs. Their understanding of sexual and reproductive health was also very limited. A study by Castro et al. in 2018 among high school students shows that young people had knowledge of sex. However, those exposed to comprehensive SRH information in schools were more likely to have positive attitudes toward contraceptives, especially condoms (58).

From the point of view of gender, it was observed that boy's knowledge with regard to self-care practices was limited to the use of condoms, while girls were more aware of self-care interventions for SRH. Young people in our study were not aware of hormone therapy for gender affirmation. Only professionals and those belonging to the LGBT community had this knowledge.

One study shows that when condoms were provided by the Secretaría de Salud, Mexico City, they were available in 94.9 percent of the health centers. In drug stores, hotels and motels, self-service shops, bars, and nightclubs, the availability of condoms was 100 percent, 82.9 percent, 75 percent, and 1.2 percent, respectively (59). This supports findings from our study, which shows that young people preferred to use condoms during intercourse because they are easily accessible. Another study showed that increased access to and use of condoms among youth was due to condom availability programs (CAPs). Yet, another study points out that adolescents have restricted access to condoms, especially in more conservative cultures and countries with poorer economies (60). These findings indicate that there is a direct association between the preference for condoms among the young population in Mexico and the availability of condoms in the state as a subsidized method of preventing HIV/STIs and unwanted pregnancies.

Contraceptive decision-making is affected by social factors (individual, interpersonal, and societal). A study published in the Lancet on contraceptive use in Latin America and the Caribbean in 2019 showed that Mexico is the only country where women are adopting long-acting contraceptive methods (61). Access to contraception also varies by gender and sexual practice (60). Young people avoided using birth-control pills for fear of side-effects. Most preferred condoms to long-term contraceptives.

Cultural beliefs and attitudes also affect SRH practices of rural and urban women in Mexico. Girls are advised to undertake or not to undertake certain activities while menstruating (62). Other social and economic barriers exacerbate existing challenges to SRHR. In 2020, a study by UNAM (Universidad Nacional Autónoma de México) showed how poverty affected millions of people in Mexico, especially women. Access to menstrual products has been a challenge for millions of girls and women in Mexico. According to UNICEF, 43 percent of adolescent girls skipped school during their menstrual period, which creates an additional barrier to learning, affecting long-term social participation and generating inequality among women in Mexico (63). The Borgen Project report showed that about 56 million people in Mexico lived below the poverty line and did not have the resources to manage their monthly menstruation. Taboos about menstruation, maintaining menstrual hygiene, and disposing of sanitary products are other important factors (64). Our study highlighted some of these factors, including the linkage between culture and the use of menstrual and contraceptive products. However, we could not find any literature that showed the correlation between cultural beliefs and the use of sanitary napkins, tampons, and menstrual cups.

One study showed that participants believed that HPV self-sampling was easy to perform and had benefits. It was convenient to screen from home and not have to travel (65). Our study also showed that young people had similar beliefs regarding self-sampling. Another study on Mexican women's attitudes and acceptability of HPV self-sampling also showed that women prefer self-testing for HPV detection (66). There is little literature on self-testing and self-management of HIV among young populations in Mexico. Our study showed that high school students in Mexico had very little knowledge and awareness about self-sampling and self-testing.

According to one study, in Mexico, about 28 to 30 percent of youth were engaged in sexual activity, with more among boys than girls and more among older adolescents than younger adolescents (67). Most participants, approximately 70 percent in our study, were sexually active. Sexual activities at an early age were higher in males. Early engagement in sexual activities was associated with high-risk behavior. Data from our study showed that sexually active girls were more aware of SRH and were also more inclined to practice contraception.

In a country like Mexico, where access to contraception is granted by law (36) and sexual education is integrated into school curricula, one would think that contraceptive use would be widespread across all ages(68)(34)(69). Yet, Mexico had one of the highest adolescent pregnancy rates among 21 countries that were studied across the world (70). Only 59 percent of sexually active adolescents used contraception in Mexico (71). It is, therefore, important to improve education on sexual and reproductive rights, provide effective counseling, and ensure access to contraceptive methods to youth (72).

During the pandemic, there was a decrease in the uptake of contraceptives by young people due to their inability to meet with their partners. Girls did not face any difficulty in accessing menstrual products at dispensaries.

Self-care was impacted with the increase in mental health concerns due to a range of pandemic-induced factors and the inability to visit healthcare facilities. Despite this, young people found ways to improve their mental health. Telemedicine is now the second-best option for minor-to-moderate health problems. Young people did not feel that they were denied any medical service during the pandemic.

Concluding comments

Our study showed that while young people had some information, they lacked a comprehensive understanding of SRH. Males are involved in sexual practices at an earlier age. They engage in risky sexual behaviors due to a lack of awareness about self-care interventions, which results in STIs. Females are more responsible in practicing self-care interventions for sexual and reproductive health and are more proactive in managing their health. The use of contraceptive methods is limited to condoms and birth control pills. Awareness and accessibility seem to be issues for other contraceptive methods. The government should develop strategies to increase the availability of condoms and other contraceptives.

Practicing risky sexual behavior and having little knowledge about self-sampling and self-testing among young people are concerns. There is a need to motivate them to adopt and practice self-care interventions such as STI testing kits at home. There is also a need to generate awareness among young people by organizing regular campaigns in schools and university campuses.

There is a need for more research to address the broad spectrum of sexual and reproductive health problems faced by young people. There is a need to better understand how improving knowledge is linked to changing their behaviors. Education is key but not sufficient for bringing about behavior change. Further research could help us to understand better the complex interactions between education and other factors that are at play in different social and cultural contexts.

Acknowledgments

The authors thank Ivan Ransom, Youth Mentor and Sustainability Ambassador, Kevin Morales Munstermann, Finance and Enterprise Mentor, and Sakthi Jeykumar, Researcher, IPN (Instituto Politécnico Nacional), Mexico for their help in data collection and for their support in reaching the targeted groups. We thank them for all their support in this research endeavor.

References

1. World Health Organization. Expanding access to health services with self-care interventions. World Health Organization. 2019 Jun 24. https://www.who.int/news/item/24-06-2019-expanding-access-to-health-services-with-self-care-interventions

2. World Health Organization. Self-care for health and well-being. World Health Organization. 2024 Apr 26. https://www.who.int/news-room/fact-sheets/detail/self-care-health-interventions

3. World Health Organization. WHO consolidated guideline on self-care interventions for health: Sexual and reproductive health and rights. Geneva: World Health Organization. 2019. http://www.ncbi.nlm.nih.gov/books/NBK544164/

4. World Health Organization. Sexual and reproductive health and rights: Infographic snapshot: Mexico 2021. World Health Organization. 2021. https://iris.who.int/handle/10665/349598

5. Morris JL & Rushwan H. Adolescent sexual and reproductive health: The global challenges. International Journal of Gynaecology and Obstetrics: The Official Organ of the International Federatio of Gynaecology and Obstetrics. 2015 Oct;131(1):40-42. https://pubmed.ncbi.nlm.nih.gov/26433504/

6. Ahmed F, Ahmad G, Brand T & Zeeb H. Key indicators for appraising

adolescent sexual and reproductive health in South Asia: International expert consensus exercise using the Delphi technique. Global Health Action;13(1):18 30555. https://www.ncbi.nlm.nih.gov/pmc/articles/PMC7594874/

7. Villa G. Adolescent pregnancy in Mexico: A growing problem fuelled by inequity. ISGLOBAL. 2019 Mar 26. https://www.isglobal.org/en/healt hisglobal/-/custom-blog-portlet/embarazo-adolescente-en-mexico-un-problema-creciente-alimentado-por-la-inequidad/5083982/9703

8. de Castro F, Rojas-Martínez R, Villalobos-Hernández A, Allen-Leigh B, Breverman-Bronstein A, Billings DL, et al. Sexual and reproductive health outcomes are positively associated with comprehensive sexual education exposure in Mexican high-school students. PLoS ONE. 2018 Mar 19;13(3):e0193780. https://www.ncbi.nlm.nih.gov/pmc/articles/PMC58588 48/

9. Juarez, F., Palma, J. L., Singh, S., & Bankole, A. Las Necesidades de Salud Sexual y Reproductiva de las Adolescentes en Mexico: Retos y Oportunidades. New York: Guttmacher Institut. 2010. https://www.scirp.org/reference/refe rencespapers?referenceid=2360202

10. Allen-Leigh B, Villalobos-Hernández A & Hernández-Serrato MI. Onset of sexual life, contraceptive use and family planning in adolescent and adult women in Mexico. Salud Pública México. 2013 Mar 4;55(Supl.2):235. http://sa ludpublica.mx/index.php/spm/article/view/5120

11. INEGI. Consultation of sociodemographic and economic indicators by geographic area. National Institute of Statistics and Geography. https://ww w.inegi.org.mx/default.html

12. Cruz P. Mexico wants to prevent teenage pregnancies. D+C - Development + Cooperation. 2023. https://www.dandc.eu/en/article/what-young-latin-americans-must-learn-about-sex-and-reproductive-health

13. Villa G. Adolescent pregnancy in Mexico: A growing problem fuelled by inequity. ISGLOBAL. 2019 Mar 26. https://www.isglobal.org/en/healt hisglobal/-/custom-blog-portlet/embarazo-adolescente-en-mexico-un-problema-creciente-alimentado-por-la-inequidad/5083982/9703

14. Darney BG, Fuentes-Rivera E, Saavedra-Avendano B, Sanhueza-Smith P, & Schiavon R. Preventing first births among adolescents in Mexico City's

public abortion programme. BMJ Sexual and Reproductive Health. 2021 Jul;47(3):e9. https://www.ncbi.nlm.nih.gov/pmc/articles/PMC8292592/

15. OECD. Comparative child well-being across the OECD. Paris: OECD. 2009 Aug; 21–63. https://www.oecd-ilibrary.org/social-issues-migration-health/doing-better-for-children/comparative-child-well-being-across-the-oecd_9789264059344-4-en

16. World Bank. Adolescent fertility rate (births per 1,000 women ages 15-19) - Middle income. World Bank. https://data.worldbank.org/indicator/SP.ADO.TFRT?locations=XP

17. Ortiz-Ortega A, García De La Torre G, Galván F, Cravioto P, Paz F, Díaz-Olavarrieta C, et al. Abortion, contraceptive use, and adolescent pregnancy among first-year medical students at a major public university in Mexico City. Rev Panam Salud Pública. 2003 Aug;14(2):125–130. http://www.scielosp.org/scielo.php?script=sci_arttext&pid=S1020-49892003000700008&lng=en&nrm=iso&tlng=en

18. Kostrzewa K. The sexual and reproductive health of young people in Latin America: Evidence from WHO case studies.SciElO 2008 Feb (50):1. https://www.scielo.org.mx/scielo.php?script=sci_arttext&pid=S0036-363 42008000100007

19. World Health Organization. Medical management of abortion. World Health Organization. 2018. https://iris.who.int/bitstream/handle/10665/278968/9789241550406-eng.pdf

20. Nove A, Matthews Z, Neal S, & Camacho AV. Maternal mortality in adolescents compared with women of other ages: Evidence from 144 countries. Lancet Global Health. 2014 Mar 01;2(3):e155–64. https://www.thelancet.com/journals/langlo/article/PIIS2214-109X(13)70179-7/fulltext#tbl5

21. Gore FM, Bloem PJ, Patton GC, Ferguson J, Joseph V, Coffey C, et al. Global burden of disease in young people aged 10–24 years: A systematic analysis. The Lancet. 2011 Jun 18;377(9783):2093–2102. https://www.thelancet.com/journals/lancet/article/PIIS0140-6736(11)60512-6/abstract

22. United Nations. The Millennium Development Goals Report 2014. United Nations. https://www.un.org/millenniumgoals/2014%20MDG%20r

eport/MDG%202014%20English%20web.pdf

23. WHO Data. Global strategy for women's, children's and adolescents' health data portal. World Health Organization. https://platform.who.int/data/maternal-newborn-child-adolescent-ageing/mca/global-strategy

24. Guttmacher. The sexual and reproductive health needs of very young adolescents in developing countries. Guttmacher Institute. 2017 May. https://www.guttmacher.org/fact-sheet/srh-needs-very-young-adolescents-in-developing-countries

25. Darroch JE, Woog V, Bankole A & Ashford LS. Adding it up: Costs and benefits of meeting the contraceptive needs of adolescents. 2016 May 05. https://www.guttmacher.org/report/adding-it-meeting-contraceptive-needs-of-adolescents

26. Sebunya RN, Boopa M, Nguyen D, Ligon L. Disparities in accessing sexual and reproductive health services and rights among adolescents and young people during COVID-19 pandemic: Culture, economic, and gender perspectives. Current Tropical Medicine Reports. 2022 Dec 01;9(4):234–242. https://doi.org/10.1007/s40475-022-00274-5

27. Castillo-Arcos L del C, Alvarez-Aguirre A, Bañuelos-Barrera Y, Valle-Solís MO, Valdez-Montero C, Kantún-Marín MA de J, et al. Edad, género y resiliencia en la conducta sexual de riesgo para its en adolescentes al sur de México. Enferm Glob. 2017;16(45):168–87. https://scielo.isciii.es/scielo.php?script=sci_abstract&pid=S1695-61412017000100168&lng=es&nrm=iso&tlng=es

28. Chesson HW, Mayaud P, & Aral SO. Sexually transmitted infections: Impact and cost-effectiveness of prevention. Major Infectious Diseases. National Center for Biotechnology Information Bookshelf. 2017. https://www.ncbi.nlm.nih.gov/books/NBK525195/

29. Reis LF, Surkan PJ, Atkins K, Garcia-Cerde R & Sanchez ZM. Risk factors for early sexual intercourse in adolescence: A systematic review of cohort studies. Child Psychiatry Human Development. 2023 Mar 25;1–14. https://www.ncbi.nlm.nih.gov/pmc/articles/PMC10039773/

30. World Health Organization. Preventing early pregnancy and poor reproductive outcomes among adolescents in developing countries. World

Health Organization. 2011 Jan 01. https://www.who.int/publications/i/item/9789241502214

31. Ganchimeg T, Ota E, Morisaki N, Laopaiboon M, Lumbiganon P, Zhang J, et al. Pregnancy and childbirth outcomes among adolescent mothers: A World Health Organization multicountry study. BJOG: An International Journal of Obstetrics and Gynaecology. 2014 Mar;121(1):40–8. https://pubmed.ncbi.nlm.nih.gov/24641534/

32. SciELO. Public health in numbers: Metrics. Scientific Electronic Library Online. https://www.scielosp.org/

33. Horizons. Programming for HIV prevention in Mexican schools. Horizons. 2003. https://healtheducationresources.unesco.org/sites/default/files/resources/Mexsum.pdf

34. Juarez F, Gayet C & Mejia-Pailles G. Factors associated with unmet need for contraception in Mexico: Evidence from the National Survey of Demographic Dynamics 2014. BMC Public Health. 2018 Apr 24;18(1):546. https://doi.org/10.1186/s12889-018-5439-0

35. Kessler K, Goldenberg SM, & Quezeda L.Contraceptive use, unmet need for contraception, and unintended pregnancy in a context of Mexico-U.S. Migration and Health. Field Actions Science Reports. 2010 (2). https://journals.openedition.org/factsreports/534

36. Rogelio Z-G, Jesus Eduardo G-F, Ahmed A A-G, et. al. Mental health stressors in higher education instructors and students in Mexico during the emergency remote teaching implementation due to COVID-19. Frontiers. 2021 Jun 14. https://www.frontiersin.org/journals/education/articles/10.3389/feduc.2021.670400/full

37. Gaibay RZ, Fagoaga EG, Asadi A, et. al. Mental health stressors in higher education instructors and students in Mexico during the emergency remote teaching implementation due to COVID-19. Frontiers in Education. 2021 Jun. https://www.researchgate.net/publication/352375982_Mental_Health_Stressors_in_Higher_Education_Instructors_and_Students_in_Mexico_During_the_Emergency_Remote_Teaching_Implementation_due_to_COVID-19

38. Singh S, Roy D, Sinha K, Parveen S, Sharma G & Joshi G. Impact of

COVID-19 and lockdown on mental health of children and adolescents: A narrative review with recommendations. Psychiatry Research. 2020 Nov; 293:113429. https://www.ncbi.nlm.nih.gov/pmc/articles/PMC7444649/

39. Zapata Garibay R, Gonzalez Fagoaga E, Asadi A, Martinez-Alvarado J, Chavez-Baray S, López I, et al. Mental health stressors in higher education instructors and students in mexico during the emergency remote teaching implementation due to COVID-19. Frontiers. 2021 Jun 14; 6:670400. https://www.frontiersin.org/journals/education/articles/10.3389/feduc.2021.670400/full

40. Kshirsagar MM, Dodamani AS, Dodamani GA, Khobragade VR & Deokar RN. Impact of COVID-19 on mental health: An overview. Reviews on Recent Clinical Trials. 2021;16(3):227–31. https://www.eurekaselect.com/article/113056

41. Rajkumar RP. COVID-19 and mental health: A review of the existing literature. Asian Journal of Psychiatry. 2020 Aug; 52:102066. https://www.ncbi.nlm.nih.gov/pmc/articles/PMC7151415/

42. Hernández-Díaz Y, Genis-Mendoza AD, Ramos-Méndez MÁ, Juárez-Rojop IE, Tovilla-Zárate CA, González-Castro TB, et al. Mental health impact of the COVID-19 pandemic on Mexican population: A systematic review. International Journal of Environmental Research and Public Health. 2022 Jun 06;19(11):6953. https://www.ncbi.nlm.nih.gov/pmc/articles/PMC9180045/

43. Ibarra-Nava I, Cardenas-de la Garza JA, Ruiz-Lozano RE & Salazar-Montalvo RG. Mexico and the COVID-19 response. Disaster Medicine and Public Health Preparedness. 2020 Jul 27;1–2. https://www.ncbi.nlm.nih.gov/pmc/articles/PMC7445449/

44. Hoehn-Velasco L, Silverio-Murillo A, Balmori de la Miyar JR & Penglase J. The impact of the COVID-19 recession on Mexican households: Evidence from employment and time use for men, women, and children. Review of Economics of the Household. 2022; 20(3):763–797. https://www.ncbi.nlm.nih.gov/pmc/articles/PMC8799985/

45. Zamarro G & Prados MJ. Gender differences in couples' division of childcare, work and mental health during COVID-19. Review of Economics of the Household. 2021 Mar 01;19(1):11–40. https://doi.org/10.1007/s11150-

020-09534-7

46. Hoehn-Velasco L, Silverio-Murillo A, Balmori de la Miyar JR & Penglase J. The impact of the COVID-19 recession on Mexican households: Evidence from employment and time use for men, women, and children. Review of Economics of the Household. 2022 Sep 01;20(3):763–97. https://doi.org/10.1007/s11150-022-09600-2

47. Domínguez-González AD, Guzmán-Valdivia G, Ángeles-Téllez FS, Manjarrez-Ángeles MA & Secín-Diep R. Depression and suicidal ideation in Mexican medical students during COVID-19 outbreak. A longitudinal study. Heliyon. 2022 Feb 01;8(2):e08851. https://www.ncbi.nlm.nih.gov/pmc/articles/PMC8806407/

48. Özdin S & Bayrak Özdin Ş. Levels and predictors of anxiety, depression and health anxiety during COVID-19 pandemic in Turkish society: The importance of gender. The International Journal of Social Psychiatry. 2020 Aug;66(5):504–11. https://pubmed.ncbi.nlm.nih.gov/32380879/

49. Ribeiro FS, Santos FH, Anunciação L, Barrozo L, Landeira-Fernandez J, Leist AK. Exploring the Frequency of Anxiety and Depression Symptoms in a Brazilian Sample during the COVID-19 Outbreak. Int J Environ Res Public Health [Internet]. 2021 May 1 [cited 2024 Aug 22];18(9):4847. Available from: https://www.ncbi.nlm.nih.gov/pmc/articles/PMC8125231/

50. Pedraz-Petrozzi B, Krüger-Malpartida H, Arevalo-Flores M, Salmavides-Cuba F, Anculle-Arauco V & Dancuart-Mendoza M. Emotional impact on health personnel, medical students, and general population samples during the COVID-19 pandemic in Lima, Peru. Revista Colombia de Psiquiatr (English Edition). 2021;50(3):189–198. https://www.ncbi.nlm.nih.gov/pmc/articles/PMC8448287/

51. Huang Y & Zhao N. Generalized anxiety disorder, depressive symptoms and sleep quality during COVID-19 outbreak in China: a web-based cross-sectional survey. Psychiatry Research. 2020 Jun; 288:112954. https://www.ncbi.nlm.nih.gov/pmc/articles/PMC7152913/

52. Czepczor-Bernat K, Swami V, Modrzejewska A, Modrzejewska J. COVID-19-Related stress and anxiety, body mass index, eating disorder symptomatology, and body image in women from Poland: A Cluster Analysis

Approach. Nutrients. 2021 Apr 20;13(4):1384. https://www.ncbi.nlm.nih.gov/pmc/articles/PMC8073902/

53. Muro A, Feliu-Soler A & Castellà J. Psychological impact of COVID-19 lockdowns among adult women: the predictive role of individual differences and lockdown duration. Women Health. Universitat Autonoma de Barcelona. 2021 Aug;61(7):668–79. https://portalrecerca.uab.cat/en/publications/psychological-impact-of-covid-19-lockdowns-among-adult-women-the-

54. Ahmed MZ, Ahmed O, Aibao Z, Hanbin S, Siyu L & Ahmad A. Epidemic of COVID-19 in China and associated Psychological Problems. Asian Journal of Psychiatry. 2020 Jun;51:102092. https://www.ncbi.nlm.nih.gov/pmc/articles/PMC7194662/

55. Glowacz F& Schmits E. Psychological distress during the COVID-19 lockdown: The young adults most at risk. Psychiatry Research. 2020 Nov;293:113486. https://www.ncbi.nlm.nih.gov/pmc/articles/PMC7518205/

56. Women Matter Mexico 2022. Lights and shadows of the pandemic. McKinsey & Company. 2022 Aug. https://www.mckinsey.com/~/media/mckinsey/featured%20insights/diversity%20and%20inclusion/women%20matter%20mexico%202022%20lights%20and%20shadows%20of%20the%20pandemic/women-matter-mexico-2022-lights-and-shadows-of-the-pandemic.pdf

57. UNFPA and Women Enabled International. The impact of COVID-19 on women and girls with disabilities. United Nations Population Fund. 2021 Jun 14:68. https://www.unfpa.org/featured-publication/impact-covid-19-women-and-girls-disabilities

58. Castro F de, Rojas-Martínez R, Villalobos-Hernández A, Allen-Leigh B, Breverman-Bronstein A, Billings DL, et al. Sexual and reproductive health outcomes are positively associated with comprehensive sexual education exposure in Mexican high-school students. PLoS ONE. 2018;13(3). https://www.ncbi.nlm.nih.gov/pmc/articles/PMC5858848/

59. Hernández-Girón C, Cruz-Valdez A, Quiterio-Trenado M, Avila-Burgos L, Peruga A & Hernández-Avila M. Availability of condoms in Mexico City. Ginecologia y Obstetricia de Mexico. 2001 Dec; 69:462–467. https://eurekamag.com/research/045/340/045340345.php?srsltid=AfmBOoqjCWoXdGjiH-

GdkocywHEktHoMblkNpc_3bF9X2QknIqiAa3T6

60. Zellner JA, Martinez-Donate AP, Hovell MF, Sipan CL, Blumberg EJ, Carrizosa CM, et al. Feasibility and use of school-based condom availability programs in Tijuana, Mexico. AIDS Behavior. 2006 Nov 01;10(6):649–657. https://doi.org/10.1007/s10461-006-9105-7

61. Leon RGP de, Ewerling F, Serruya SJ, Silveira MF, Sanhueza A, Moazzam A, et al. Contraceptive use in Latin America and the Caribbean with a focus on long-acting reversible contraceptives: prevalence and inequalities in 23 countries. Lancet Global Health. 2019 Feb 01;7(2):e227–235. https://www.th elancet.com/journals/langlo/article/PIIS2214-109X(18)30481-9/fulltext

62. Marvan ML & Trujillo P. Menstrual socialization, beliefs, and attitudes concerning menstruation in rural and urban Mexican women. Health Care for Women International. 2010 Jan;31(1):53–67. https://www.researchgate.net/publication/43135634_Menstrual_Socialization_Beliefs_and_Attitudes_Concerning_Menstruation_in_Rural_and_Urban_Mexican_Women#fullTextFileContent

63. Bello M. Menstruation: Growing public health matter in Mexico. Mexico Business. 2021 Mar 03. https://mexicobusiness.news/health/news/menstruation-growing-public-health-matter-mexico

64. Philipp J. Period poverty in Mexico. The Borgen Project. 2021. https://borgenproject.org/period-poverty-in-mexico/

65. Kamath Mulki A, Withers M. Human Papilloma Virus self-sampling performance in low- and middle-income countries. BMC Womens Health. 2021 Jan 06;21(1):12. Available from: https://doi.org/10.1186/s12905-020-01158-4

66. Rodriguez GMG, Ornelas OAO, Champion JD, et. al. Attitude and acceptability of the self-sampling in HPV carrier women. Sage Journals. 2022 (20):1. https://journals.sagepub.com/doi/abs/10.1177/15404153211001577?journalCode=hcia

67. Gutiérrez JP & Atienzo EE. Socioeconomic status, urbanicity and risk behaviors in Mexican youth: an analysis of three cross-sectional surveys. BMC Public Health. 2011 Nov 30.;11:900. https://www.ncbi.nlm.nih.gov/pmc/articles/PMC3260336/

68. Cuadernillo. Situacion de la salud sexual y reproductiva. Republica Mexicana. 2016. https://www.gob.mx/cms/uploads/attachment/file/23721 6/Cuadernillo_SSR_RM.pdf

69. Rojas R, Castro F de, Villalobos A, Allen-Leigh B, Romero M, Braverman-Bronstein A, et al. Educación sexual integral: Cobertura, homogeneidad, integralidad y continuidad en escuelas de México. Salud Pública México. 2017 Jan 03;59(1, ene-feb):19–27. https://saludpublica.mx/index.php/spm/article/view/8411

70. Sedgh G, Finer LB, Bankole A, Eilers MA & Singh S. Adolescent pregnancy, birth, and abortion rates across countries: Levels and recent trends. Journal of Adolescent Health: Official Publication of the Society of Adolescent Medicine. 2015 Feb;56(2):223–230. https://pubmed.ncbi.nlm.nih.gov/25620306/

71. Hernández MF, Maria CM & Miguel S. Panorama de la salud sexual y reproductiva, 2014. Government of Mexico. 2014. https://www.gob.mx/cms/uploads/attachment/file/400135/Hern_ndez_-_Panorama_de_la_salud_sexual_y_reproductiva_2014.pdf

72. Cadernos de Saúde Pública. Escola Nacional de Saúde Pública Sergio Arouca, Fundação Oswaldo Cruz. 40(9). 2024. Vfyh7QzKLxXdyjyXBV7mvXs.pdf https://www.scielo.br/j/csp/a/Vfyh7QzKLxXdyjyXBV7mvXs/?lang=en&format=pdf

Narrative: A Young Bisexual Woman's Guide to Sexual Health Awareness and Empowerment

Pamela is a 22-year-old female who has lived in Mexico for almost her entire life. She identified herself as bisexual and expressed her openness and progressive approach to relationships and sexual health. Her first sexual relationship was with a heterosexual male who never gave importance to sexual matters that concerned her health. Like any other young woman, she navigated through the complexity of her adulthood by learning from her mistakes and educating herself. "For my ex-boyfriend, everything relating to sexual and reproductive health was not important. Whereas, for my girlfriend, it was very important. If something was right, she would tell me." Pamela's sexual experiences with both heterosexual and same-sex partners made her realize her sexual orientation. Pamela's journey represents the challenges that many young women face in Mexico.

Pamela completed her schooling at a Catholic school where providing information on sexual health was prohibited. She had very little knowledge about sexual and reproductive health (SRH) during her high school. The only source of her knowledge was government programs. At the age of 14, it was school, and at the age of 16, as a teenage adult, it was the internet from where she obtained information on contraceptives and SRH. "I used to swim. I used a tampon, which was a problem for my mom. When I turned 17, my mom got to know that I was using a menstrual cup secretly." After school, she moved to another state to study pharma, where she graduated from the university. Her mother's financial support and a scholarship enabled her to focus on her academic and career goals without economic constraints. Pamela lived with her mother, brother, and niece. Her family dynamics were supportive yet traditional. Her mother, who managed the household finances, played a significant role in decision-making, especially concerning healthcare. Despite this, Pamela asserted her independence, particularly in her educational pursuits and personal life, including making decisions related to sexual and reproductive health. She aspired to specialize in environmental sciences and was motivated to engage in the social sector.

Unlike most girls in their early twenties, Pamela had a comprehensive understanding of sexual health. She mentioned how her family influenced her sexual and reproductive health knowledge. Her grandmother's battle with uterine cancer was a lesson. "My grandma had cancer of the uterus. I wanted to be very careful about that. At the beginning of the pandemic, I had a little secretion in one of my breasts. I visited a doctor and got the blotting test for prolactin." Pamela was single but was sexually active. Sexual health to her was to get to know about your body and the process of conception, which also included care during pregnancy and getting the right kind of treatment when you fall ill. Therefore, she never hesitated to get tested for human papillomavirus and other sexually transmitted infections (STIs). "A papillomavirus test was done with the cells of the cervix. This was done through a campaign at the university. They also conducted the syphilis test with a drop of blood." Pamela was not just aware of self-care interventions for SRH, she was also aware of the right sources from which she could access them. She knew about self-sampling, self-testing, self-monitoring, and self-injecting.

As a healthcare student, Pamela was well aware of self-care interventions for SRH. Several university and internet campaigns were her main sources of information, especially about contraceptives. She was very particular about the source of information and relied only on authentic sources. Recalling her experience of being misled by the information present on the internet, she mentioned, "On Wikipedia and some blogs, the information went wrong. It was related to health. As I told you earlier about the secretion from one of my breasts, it showed breast cancer. But I found out later that it was a hormonal issue. So, now I only trust '.edu' to get information or an official logo or logo of the Mexican government."

Pamela's awareness and usage of contraceptive methods spanned male and female condoms, intrauterine devices (Cu–T), birth control pills, and emergency contraception. Advocating for mutual care and decision-making, she believes that birth control and family planning should be a shared responsibility between partners. "I think it should be a task of both partners. They should take care of each other. A girl should take birth control pills or hormones. But it is not just a task of one person." However, other than the condom, she was not sure of any other contraceptive methods that a male partner could use. Pamela had strong opinions about abortion as well and expressed her emotions and support about how it should be the decision of the woman. She mentioned, "It is a very highlighted issue in Latin America. Unfortunately, it is illegal in my state. It depends on each state in Mexico. In my state, you can have an abortion if you are a victim of rape or if the pregnancy is risky." Pamela felt more comfortable in her relationship with a female partner than a male one. She discussed self-care interventions for sexual health with her female partner. It was easy to talk to her about sex. In contrast, with her male partner, she felt controlled and pressured to some extent to behave in a certain way.

The situation during the COVID-19 pandemic brought significant changes in Pamela's life. Initially, it disrupted her routine, forcing her to return to her hometown and to adapt to online classes. The lockdown affected her family's finances, compelling them to cut out non-essential expenses and sell their personal belongings. Pamela shared household responsibilities with her mother that were overwhelming for her. "I started to clean the house and helped my mom with cooking and other household chores like taking out the trash. I used to go to get groceries and do other work. I felt good when I had to go out, but when I came back, it was stressful." The situation during the pandemic exacerbated Pamela's anxiety and depression, leading her to seek therapy. Pamela could not contact her mom or friends for counseling during that time. But when she rejoined college in March 2021, she started therapy at the college, which proved helpful. She said, "I started therapy to deal with my anxiety. I discussed my issues, and the therapist advised me on how to balance emotions and suggested some workouts. In the career class, we got a tutor who helped us with all the paperwork and motivated students and whoever asked for special attention. Therapy was free for students and professors of the university."

Due to financial constraints within her family, Pamela and her family always accessed healthcare from a government hospital. She said, "I usually go for health care with my mother. In Mexico, we have a system where she takes responsibility. Every time I need to visit, she accompanies me unless I visit a private facility. I usually visit government centers. We do not have to pay for health services there." Her reliance on government healthcare meant facing long waits and limited services, which was also one of the reasons why she could not seek counseling support from the healthcare system. She recalled the pandemic and mentioned, "It was a tough time. The idea of getting sick was terrifying. Every hospital was a COVID hospital, and private clinics were very expensive. The pharmacy stores were not allowed to sell anything without a prescription." As a bisexual, Pamela mentioned she experienced disrespect in the healthcare setting for matters related to sexual health and was judged for matters related to mental health due to the attached stigma. She said, "For me, as a bisexual woman, it was not easy to access SRH care." All these hurdles motivated her to focus on self-care, balancing her mental health with physical wellness through exercise and mindfulness practices. Pamela's use of self-care products and SRH services evolved. While some services became harder to access due to the pandemic, she adapted using online resources and community support where possible. She started viewing self-care as recognizing and addressing her emotional and physical needs.

Pamela's outlook on life was shaped by her experience of societal expectations, healthcare challenges, and personal growth. She believed in achieving her goals and overcoming challenges, which enabled her to become a strong and empowered woman with self-efficacy and resilience. Her experiences highlight the importance of education, support systems, and self-care for young women as ways to empowerment.

Self-Care Experiences of High School Students and College Graduates in India

Saroj Pachauri, Public Health Specialist, Trustee, Center for Human Progress, New Delhi, India, and Director, POP (Protect Our Planet) Movement, New York, USA

Ash Pachauri, Director, Center for Human Progress, New Delhi, India, and Senior Mentor, POP (Protect Our Planet) Movement, New York, USA

Drishya Pathak, Research Associate, Center for Human Progress, New Delhi, India and Youth Mentor, POP (Protect Our Planet) Movement, New York, USA

Komal Mittal, Research Associate, Center for Human Progress, New Delhi, India and Youth Mentor, POP (Protect Our Planet) Movement, New York, USA

Abstract

Despite advancements in healthcare, access to essential health services in India remains inadequate due to high costs, under-resourced systems, and neglect of peoples' rights. Self-care interventions are crucial for achieving Universal Health Coverage (UHC) and the Sustainable Development Goals (SDGs) on health, gender equality, and women's empowerment. In India, over 50 percent of adolescents engage in self-medication regularly. However, sociocultural norms, lack of sex education, and restrictive societal attitudes pose significant challenges to self-care, particularly for sexual and reproductive health and rights (SRHR). Young people face barriers such as stigma, misinformation, and limited access to health services, increasing risks of sexually transmitted infections (STIs) and unintended pregnancies. Integrating self-care interventions into mainstream healthcare programs can empower individuals and improve health outcomes. In this chapter, the authors examine young people's attitudes, practices, and behaviors regarding self-care interventions and highlight the need for a supportive environment to enhance self-care for SRHR.

Background

Healthcare systems have made significant progress over time. However, access to healthcare is still inadequate globally. Half of the world's population still lacks access to essential health services. There are many reasons for this gap including high cost of healthcare, under-resourced health systems, inadequate reach of services, and neglect of clients' rights (1). Self-care interventions offer the most promising strategies for achieving Universal Health Coverage (UHC) and the Sustainable Development Goals (SDGs) on health, gender equality, women's empowerment, and health service coverage worldwide (2). As mentioned in the introductory chapter, self-care interventions can be provided fully or partially outside of the formal health system with or without the support of healthcare providers. There is a need to promote self-care interventions and integrate them within the mainstream healthcare system. Self-care is not a replacement for sustainable high-quality healthcare services. Rather, it is a means of empowering and supporting individuals to manage their own health (3).

Self-medication is a common form of self-care. Studies in India show that more than 50 percent of adolescents use self-medication regularly. At the global level, self-medication is important as it provides 65-85 percent of healthcare (4)(5). During the past two decades, there has been an increase in the use of self-care interventions due to increased awareness, innovations, and technologies that have been developed for a broad range of health conditions including sexual and reproductive health, mental health, chronic diseases, and most recently, COVID-19. Self-care interventions include several drugs, devices, diagnostics, and digital tools. While the World Health Organization (WHO) recommends all self-care interventions, a special emphasis is placed on sexual and reproductive health and rights (SRHR) interventions for improving healthcare (1). Self-care interventions for SRHR are people-centered. The health system is, however, also important. Various factors govern the successful delivery of healthcare including information, accessibility, availability, affordability, quality, utilization, agency, and social support (5).

Many people around the world lack access to essential sexual and reproductive health services. Young people who are in transition from teenage to adulthood face several challenges. Risky sexual behavior in adolescents leads to health problems that are preventable. Structural factors are among the several reasons young people face such problems (6). These factors could be social, religious, economic, gender norms, and cultural beliefs. Sociocultural norms related to adolescent sexuality in India are ridden with many sexual myths and taboos. Sexual taboos that have their roots in cultural beliefs have important implications for sexual health. For example, several misconceptions about menstruation and masturbation result in marginalizing youth, especially girls and young women, who are adversely affected, and their fundamental rights are violated by discriminatory practices. They also lack control over matters related to sexuality, contraception, pregnancy, and abortion.

In addition to structural factors and fundamental rights discussed above, health system factors, including providers' attitudes and knowledge, are important for ensuring the provision of quality healthcare for young people (6). In India, there is no provision of sex education either at home or in school, and there are no health services for addressing adolescents' sexual problems. Society in India is very traditional and conservative in its outlook (7). Discussing sexual matters is forbidden. Indian parents do not discuss with their children changes in the body that occur during adolescence. There is a discomfort in sharing knowledge on sexuality (8). Therefore, boys and girls do not receive any information about the natural changes that occur in their bodies and in their minds during adolescence. There is also a discomfort in discussing premarital sex and the use of sexual and reproductive health services (9).

Our study shows that sexual and reproductive health is a major concern for youth. Age at first sex is decreasing in India. Unmarried girls are sexually active at the age of 15, and boys are sexually active at the age of 20 years and above. This difference between girls and boys is primarily because girls get married at very young ages. Pre-marital sex is socially restricted and is stigmatized in India (10). Studies show that education is a major factor for delaying the average age of first sex in both girls and boys (11). The rate of increasing premarital sex is documented in the successive National Family Health Surveys (NFHS) -3, 4, and 5.

In India, young people's access to sexual and reproductive health services is impacted by social stigma, lack of education, and legal barriers. These factors result in unmet needs for a significant number of sexually active adolescents, elevating the risk for both sexually transmitted infections (STIs), including HIV, and unintended pregnancies. Girls face greater obstacles in accessing health information and contraceptive services than boys (12). Reproductive empowerment could help young individuals and couples achieve their reproductive goals if self-care interventions are added to the existing services (13).

Our study explored young people's attitudes, practices, and behaviors regarding self-care interventions. We also examined the importance of a safe, supportive, and enabling environment for increasing the adoption of self-care interventions for sexual and reproductive health and rights.

Study methodology

A qualitative research study was undertaken in Delhi, Haryana, Uttar Pradesh, Maharashtra, Gujarat, Karnataka, Tamil Nadu, and West Bengal. Qualitative research methods allow greater spontaneity and interaction with the research participants. They provide an opportunity for the participants to respond elaborately and in greater detail, which provides a more nuanced understanding of the issues.

Data was collected online and offline by conducting in-depth interviews (IDIs), focus group discussions (FGDs), and workshops with high school students and college graduates (married and unmarried). The questionnaires were aligned with WHO's Self-care Values and Preferences Survey that was administered globally (4). However, our study included additional components on gender norms, mental health, and COVID-19.

The interviews were conducted using interview guides. They were approximately 90-120 minutes in length and audio recorded using an external device. The audio recordings were transcribed and checked for accuracy. Eight IDIs and two FGDs were conducted with high school students (14-19 years of age). Thirteen IDIs and two FGDs were conducted with college graduates (19-26 years of age). One of the research participants was bisexual, and six of the college graduates were married.

Ethical approval for undertaking the study was granted by the Institutional Review Board of Sigma (Sigma-IRB), Sigma Research and Consulting, New Delhi. Before conducting the research interviews, the interviewer described the objectives and importance of the study to all research participants. Participants were given consent forms which described the study risks and potential harm. They were assured that the study posed minimal or no quantifiable harm to their physical or mental wellbeing. They were also told they could skip any questions that they did not wish to answer and that they could withdraw consent at any point during the interview, following which the data would be destroyed. Written and verbal consent was obtained from all participants. Confidentiality of the study participants was assured. The questionnaires were translated into the local languages to suit the language preferences of the target populations.

Transcripts were thoroughly read, and some unique similarities and differences were identified in the data collected. Based on this, a number of themes were used as probes for analysis. The themes included service provision, attitudes, knowledge and behavior, scope, condom use, social support networks, empowerment, sexually transmitted infections (STIs), including HIV/AIDS, and pregnancy. Quotes were generously used to amplify the voices of the research participants and to highlight the research results.

Literature review

A literature search was carried out across multiple databases, including PubMed, British Medical Journal (BMJ), the World Health Organization (WHO), PubMed Central (PMC), Sage Journals, Science Direct, Springer, Taylor & Francis, Wiley Online Library, and others. A variety of search terms and keywords were used in this process. These included young, youth, adolescent, young adult, self-care, sexual and reproductive health, abortion, unintended pregnancy, self-sampling, self-management, mental health problems, stress, depression, suicide, alcohol, tobacco use, substance use, and violence.

Existing literature on self-care is notably sparse, particularly for young people in India. A comprehensive literature review revealed a significant lack of research focused on self-care practices related to sexual and reproductive health among youth in India. Despite the urgent need to promote self-care for sexual and reproductive health, available research is very limited. This gap underscores a critical need for further research on self-care practices, especially with regard to sexual and reproductive health and rights. Addressing this need is important for designing effective self-care interventions and improving the overall quality of healthcare.

Knowledge and practice of self-care for SRH among young people

Globally, adolescents are increasingly becoming sexually active, often without protection, which places them at risk of contracting sexually transmitted diseases (STDs), including human immunodeficiency virus (HIV). In India, adolescents (15-24 years of age) comprise about 25 percent of the total population and account for 31 percent of the AIDS burden (14). Therefore, it is crucial for individuals to learn behaviors that support their sexual and reproductive health and protect them from the adverse effects of risky sexual activities (15).

Being in a learning phase of life, adolescents often struggle to fully comprehend the dangers of unsafe, casual sex, drug abuse, and other behaviors that increase the risk of HIV transmission (14).

With over one billion young people (15-24 years) worldwide, accessing health services can be challenging due to limited educational resources and a lack of digital health content. Self-care involves conscious and deliberate actions and behaviors aimed at improving health (15). According to the concept of self-care, individuals are responsible for managing their own health and should adopt healthy behaviors to achieve the desired health outcomes (15).

Even when young people can access care, factors such as provider bias may limit their ability to receive high quality care (16). Sex education should be an integral part of the learning process from childhood through adulthood. Disparities exist between the HIV/AIDS curriculum in schools and the education that is actually provided (17). Despite this serious situation, many Indian states have banned sex education in schools due to protests from legislators. A study assessing awareness of HIV/AIDS among school children in Delhi highlighted the need to reinforce AIDS education in schools and destigmatize the attitudes of young people (18) . Awareness levels were related to the level of education. A review done by Bertrand and Anhang revealed that young people in developing countries are significantly influenced by mass media interventions on HIV/AIDS related behavior (19).

It is important to tailor self-care approaches to address young people's needs to understand their challenges and identify effective ways to reach them. Key questions to consider are: What challenges do young people face in managing their health? What do young people want the government to do to enhance self-care? And how can young people change the way they care for their health?

Sexual consent and legal age of marriage

The concept of 'age of consent' is often seen as being synonymous with 'age at marriage'. In India, the legal age for both marriage and consensual sex is 18 years, although the government is considering raising the legal age of marriage for women to 21 years (20). According to the World Population Review, the global age of consent ranges from 11 to 21 years with the most common range being between 14 and 16 years. India's age of consent at 18 years is higher than the global average which may not be beneficial (21).

Sexual intercourse before marriage is considered immoral, obscene, and against religious tenets. There is growing evidence that laws focused solely on age can have negative consequences for girls and adolescents if they are not part of a comprehensive, gender-transformative approach that supports girls' rights and is sensitive to cultural and social contexts (22). However, surveys indicate that young adults in India are increasingly engaging in sexual activities before marriage. Debates continue on whether higher legal age limits will promote gender justice or merely provide punitive solutions to complex social issues like child marriage and adolescent sex (23). The Protection of Children from Sexual Offences (POCSO) Act 2012 prohibits any sexual relationship between people under 18 and classifies such crimes within marriage as aggravated offenses (24).

Raising the age of consent without addressing underlying social issues can create legal barriers that disrupt natural biological behaviors, potentially leading to sexual perversion and secretive information seeking from unreliable sources like the internet, which can be dangerous.

Risky sexual behaviors among young people in India

Adolescence is a critical life stage characterized by profound physical, emotional, and societal transformation. Sexual behavior, a crucial aspect of adolescent development, occurs in the midst of significant physical and psychological changes. With India hosting the world's largest population of 253 million adolescents, it is important to understand the sexual behaviors of adolescents (25). Studies show that unmarried adolescent boys are more likely to engage in sexual activities compared to girls. Boys are also more likely to approve of premarital sexual relations. Additionally, boys have more unsupervised freedom, which increases their opportunities for engaging in sexual relations. Boys indulge in risky sexual behavior, including early sexual activity before the age of 18 years, and they have unprotected sex. Some also have multiple sex partners and have sex with individuals who indulge in high-risk behaviors. They have sex with drug users, exchange sex for money, and engage in anal intercourse (26). These behaviors significantly increase the risk of contracting HIV and other sexually transmitted infections.

A study by Chandra et al. in 2023 where data from the National Family Health Survey (NFHS-5) 2019–21, was analyzed, highlighted concerning statistics. Fourteen percent of young men (<18 years) engaged in early sexual activity, had unprotected sex (68%), and had multiple sexual partners (4%) (27). Premarital sexual activity was not uncommon among young people, with males exhibiting higher rates than females. Inconsistent condom use, multiple partners, and paid sex increased the risk of STIs (28).

Studies indicate that premarital sex is more common in men (15-22%) as compared to women (1-6%) (26). A study involving 2,475 never married boys and girls by Kumar *et al.* found that only 22.3 percent males and 6.3 percent females consistently used condoms during premarital sex. A study from Gujarat reported that 40 percent of males and 7.4 percent of females (15–24 years of age) had multiple sexual partners, while 32.1 percent of males and 3.2 percent of females reported having paid sex or exchanged sex for money/gifts

(26). Despite efforts, sexual health challenges persist. According to NFHS-4, HIV prevalence in India was 0.02 percent among unmarried women and 0.10 percent among unmarried men aged 15 to 24 years (29). Earlier data from the NFHS-3 (2005-06) showed that four percent of young women and 15 percent of young men engaged in premarital sex, and only 14.1 percent (14.7% urban versus 13.9% rural) unmarried, sexually active adolescent females used contraceptives (26).

Misconceptions about HIV/AIDS are widespread. A study among school going girls in Haryana revealed higher levels of awareness of these issues. Studies conducted outside India have also reported increased awareness of condom use for HIV prevention (14). School children are at risk of contracting HIV infection. A significant number of young people reported attending STI clinics in cosmopolitan cities like Pune in India (14).

Factors such as early marriage, gender inequality, and peer pressure exacerbate risky sexual behaviors, leading to significant health and societal consequences. According to a study by Ubale et al. in 2023, men are more likely to engage in multiple sexual activities than women. These differences can be attributed to education, alcohol drinking, spending more time away from home, early first sexual encounters, and domestic violence. These factors increase risky sexual behaviors among youth (30). Because of the lack of access to sexual health-related information and healthcare services, adolescents from low-income households are more susceptible to adverse outcomes. Furthermore, in poorer areas, sexuality related cultural and societal norms further complicate the problem(25). These findings underscore the high prevalence of risky sexual behaviors among young people in India. Serious efforts are needed to reduce the incidence of HIV and other STIs. Comprehensive sex education, coupled with improved access to healthcare services and interventions targeting social and economic inequalities, should be prioritized.

Addressing unintended pregnancy and abortion concerns

A 2016 study by the Guttmacher Institute and the World Health Organization (WHO) revealed that an estimated 56 million abortions were performed globally each year between 2010 and 2014, highlighting the importance of providing safe abortion services (30).

Unintended pregnancies, especially among adolescents, pose significant public health problems across countries (31). As adolescents constitute a large part of India's population, they face this challenge amidst factors such as age, religion, socioeconomic status, accessibility of contraceptives, and knowledge of contraceptive use (31)(32). This is a global issue that not only impacts women but also their families and the society. Unplanned pregnancies among adolescent girls often result from either not using family planning methods or using them incorrectly or being forced into sexual activities. Several factors contribute to adolescent pregnancy. A significant factor is the lack of access to and utilization of modern contraceptive methods. Societal norms require women to showcase fertility to validate their worth (33)(34).

Research in 2015 showed that nearly half of India's pregnancies were un-intended, with one-third ending in abortion, amounting to approximately 15.6 million abortions annually. Such unintended pregnancies, especially in developing countries, lead to grave health consequences due to associated poverty, malnutrition, lack of education, and poor sanitation (35)(36).

In India, a significant number of women marry early and start bearing children between the ages of 15 and 19. Approximately 3.4 million adolescent girls express a desire to avoid pregnancy. This includes 3.2 million married girls and 195,000 sexually active unmarried girls (37). Abortion has been legal in India since 1971. The Medical Termination of Pregnancy Act (MTP Act) permits pregnancy terminations up to 20 weeks of gestation under various circumstances, including situations where it is necessary to save the woman's life and/or protect her physical or mental health as well as in cases of economic and social necessity, rape, contraceptive failure among married girls, and fetal anomalies (30). Unlike many other countries, India did not face any significant obstacles such as religious fanaticism, pseudo bioethics, judicial biases, or political conservatism when enacting the MTP Act (38). Of the two million pregnancies occurring among adolescents in India annually, approximately 53 percent result in abortion, totaling 930,000 abortions annually. Unfortunately, an estimated 78 percent of abortions among adolescents are unsafe (39).

In India, the widespread misuse of the abortion pill mifepristone has led to a significant number of women ending up in hospital emergency wards (40). A 2014 study by Nivedita et al. found that 31 percent of abortion patients had attempted to terminate their pregnancies using abortion pills on their own (40). This misuse is contributing to a worrying trend including an almost 50 percent increase in teen pregnancies in Gurgaon, India over the last 4-5 years (41). Annually, about 10 million Indian women terminate pregnancies with abortion pills, often without any medical oversight, posing several health risks (42). This situation is due to a combination of factors such as lack of education and awareness about legal and safe options for abortion, risks associated with medical abortion, the desire for confidentiality, affordability, and the unrestricted availability of these drugs. Healthcare professionals are calling for enhancing public education on the safe use of abortion pills (40).

Despite legal provisions, many adolescents still undergo unsafe abortion procedures. One study indicated that only 31 percent of abortions followed the MTP guidelines. The stigma around unintended pregnancy, especially for unmarried women, leads to delayed pregnancy disclosure and reliance on non-formal and/or self-managed abortions. This is due to concerns regarding confidentiality and other barriers such as lack of mobility and financial constraints (43)(44)(45)(46)(47).

Interventions aimed at preventing adolescent pregnancies, particularly those that focus on primary prevention strategies within schools—aiming to avert unintended pregnancies from the outset—have shown promise in lowering teenage pregnancy rates. Such interventions not only increase the use of contraceptives but also improve attitudes and knowledge and delay initiating sexual activity (48). Prevention efforts must address the economic, sociocultural, and environmental factors that place adolescents at risk of dealing with an unintended pregnancy. For these interventions to be successful, they must be implemented in a manner that guarantees adolescent girls' access to critical health services. There is also a need to address individual-level factors such as education and self-esteem for girls to take charge of their sexual health and make informed choices.

With the growing demand for medical abortion and its self-administration in India, coupled with the willingness of both clients and providers to embrace health technology, there is a clear inclination to use telemedicine for providing abortion services. Challenges in public sector abortion provision, such as limited trained personnel, lack of equipment, and judgmental attitudes, underscore the need for alternative solutions (49). Telemedicine offers a promising avenue to bridge these gaps. It provides safe abortion care while reducing the strain on the healthcare infrastructure by minimizing in-person visits and ensuring client privacy and confidentiality. By expanding telemedicine to include medical abortion, India can pioneer accessible and safe abortion services (49).

In a study conducted by Dattatraya and Sekher, risky sexual behavior and several other characteristics of youth aged 15-29 were analyzed. The source of data used for the study was the National Family Health Survey conducted from 2019 to 2021. This study found that unmarried men were involved more than unmarried women in risky sexual practices such as having multiple sexual partners and using the withdrawal method during intercourse. These results were consistent across socioeconomic and demographic characteristics (50). This study also showed that low education, spending more time away from home, alcohol drinking, early age at first sexual encounter, behavior of the father, and other gender norms affected sexual and reproductive health. The increase in premarital sex highlights the need for providing SRH-related information and services to youth, irrespective of their age and marital status. A study conducted by Singh I. et al. in 2021 revealed that the use of modern contraceptives among married adolescents increased from four percent in 1992-93 to 10 percent in 2015−16 (51). In 2021, 71 percent of adolescents who wanted to avoid pregnancy had an unmet need for modern contraception compared to 27 percent of all women of reproductive age (39).

Socioeconomic and cultural barriers

Adolescents in India generally have a superficial level of understanding of sexual matters due to social taboos and stigma that surround sex education. Despite rapid social and economic changes, conversations about sex education remain shrouded in silence, leaving many without adequate guidance on relationships and intimacy. Prevailing cultural norms, particularly those emphasizing premarital chastity for girls, significantly restrict their decision-making in sexual relationships.

A United Nations report indicates that approximately four million young people in India are HIV infected—making the country one of the high-risk areas for HIV. Unfortunately, most of these individuals belong to the most productive age group. The percentage of those receiving treatment is low due to social stigma and the threat of discrimination (14).

Access to comprehensive information and services is particularly limited in rural and low-income areas. Factors such as early marriage, gender inequality, peer pressure, and exposure to domestic violence result in increased risky sexual behaviors among youth. Men are consistently more likely to engage in multiple sexual activities across various demographic and socioeconomic backgrounds. Low education, alcohol consumption, and witnessing parental violence amplify the risk.

Despite the legalization of abortion, barriers such as stigma persist, leading many women to self-manage abortion by obtaining medication from pharmacists (52). Ensuring access to reliable contraception and culturally-sensitive reproductive healthcare services, including emergency contraception, is crucial for addressing high maternal mortality ratios (36). Self-care offers an opportunity to engage with the health system in an equitable, affordable, safe, private, and confidential manner, without the fear of stigma (16).

Use of contraceptives

Due to social norms, the sexual and reproductive health of all sexually active youth, married and unmarried, is an important issue in India. Over the last three decades, there has been growing evidence that corroborates the increasing involvement of youth in premarital sex. Most adolescents begin sexual activity without adequate knowledge about sexuality or contraception or protection from STIs/HIV. Between NFHS-1 (1992-1993) and NFHS-4 (2014-2015), the use of condoms and pills among youth aged 15-19 years increased notably while the use of intrauterine devices (IUDs) remained unchanged. The use of contraceptive methods has increased as per the latest NFHS-5 (2019-2021) (53). Reliance on traditional contraceptive methods among married adolescents increased from four percent in NFHS-1 to six percent in NFHS-3 (2005-2006), but it declined to five percent in NFHS-4. Despite this, in the NFHS-4 survey, 10 percent of adolescents opted for modern contraceptive methods. Five percent continued to rely on traditional methods, which are considered to be less effective.

Generating awareness about contraceptive methods among youth is impacted by stigma, including stigma among service providers. A qualitative study conducted by Shukla A et al. that explored the attitudes of healthcare providers showed that almost a quarter of the providers were either hesitant or were against providing contraceptives to unmarried youth. They had strong personal views regarding premarital sex. They were also concerned about the negative reactions of the community if they recommended contraceptives for unmarried youth. They, therefore, hesitated to provide contraceptives to unmarried youth (54).

The most reliable method for preventing unwanted pregnancies is to abstain from sexual intercourse. The American Academy of Pediatrics (AAP) recommends that parents should talk with their adolescents about abstinence (not having sexual intercourse) as well as other contraceptives, including condoms. In the case of sexually active adolescents, using effective contraceptives such as condoms, birth control pills, the patch, the vaginal ring, the intrauterine device(IUD), and injectable birth control methods significantly lower the risk of unwanted pregnancy (55). Oral contraceptives that contain levonorgestrel, a progestin, are recognized for their effectiveness as emergency contraceptives. When taken within 72 hours after unprotected sex, they significantly lower the risk of pregnancy. Now packaged as emergency contraception pills, they are noted for their efficacy (56).

Only about one million (29%) adolescents in India who wanted to avoid pregnancy were currently using modern contraceptive methods. According to the Guttmacher Institute, if all adolescent girls desiring to avoid pregnancy had access to modern contraceptives, comprehensive counseling, information, and the full range of contraceptive options, and if all maternal, newborn, and abortion-related healthcare needs were met, there would be 732,000 fewer unintended pregnancies and 482,000 fewer unsafe abortions annually (39).

Between 1995 and 2020, there was an increase from 36 percent to 60 percent of adolescent girls whose family planning needs were met through modern contraceptives in India. However, despite this improvement, one in four adolescent girls aged 15–19 who wanted to prevent pregnancy still did not use a modern contraceptive method (57). This was because of various factors, including contraceptive failure, lack of access to adolescent-friendly SRH services, lack of access to contraceptive services, and sexual assault and rape. Unwanted pregnancies carry stigma and force individuals to make difficult decisions regarding parenting, adoption, and abortion (58)(59)(60)(61).

Approximately 48 percent of adolescent girls and their partners using modern contraceptives rely on male condoms. Another 40 percent use other short-acting methods with 37 percent opting for oral contraceptive pills, and three percent depending on injectables, lactational amenorrhea, or female condoms. These methods are mainly sourced from the private sector. Additionally, eight percent of adolescent women using modern contraceptives had undergone permanent female sterilization, while four percent used long-acting reversible methods (39).

Condom use varies across India, with higher rates in the central and western regions than in the south (62). Correct and consistent use of condoms is crucial not only for preventing pregnancy but also for reducing the risk of HIV and other sexually transmitted infections (STIs) (63). Despite this, barriers such as partner rejection, perceived discomfort, and lack of satisfaction with condoms, alongside issues like alcohol use by partners, depression, anxiety, and unavailability, hinder their use (64).

In 2014, a study by Jain et al. surveyed 375 students aged 13-15 years in central India. It revealed that there was a mixed awareness of contraceptive methods. While 49 percent had heard about some form of contraception, 51 percent were fully unaware of contraception. Among those with knowledge of contraception, 38.7 percent knew about condoms and 23.5 percent were aware of oral contraceptive pills. But knowledge about emergency contraception was very low. Females were more aware of oral contraceptives and emergency contraception compared to males (65).

Data from the NFHS-4 Survey underscored the urgency of addressing gaps in reproductive and sexual health. NFHS-4 indicated that nearly 80 percent of men aged 20-24 years had not used contraception during their last sexual encounter (66). NFHS 5 showed a slight increase in condom use among men from 5.6 to 9.5 percent, while sterilization remained the predominant form of contraception for women (67). Although 82 percent of the men knew that condoms could prevent HIV/AIDS, misconceptions persisted, affecting their acceptance, especially by married men (68). Limited access to reproductive health services, particularly in rural areas, and the social stigma around purchasing condoms posed significant barriers, as was highlighted by a study by the Population Council in New Delhi (68). This study showed that many young people's pre-marital sexual experiences were unprotected due to these challenges, underscoring the need for improved access to contraception and sexual health information (68).

To address these issues, the World Health Organization (WHO) recommends self-testing products such as HIV self-testing (HIVST) kits as a crucial strategy for addressing gaps in HIV diagnosis among key populations such as sex workers, LGBTQ+, drug users, and prisoners (69)(70). Globally, 98 countries now have policies supportive of HIVST, and 52 have actively implemented them. Many countries, including India, have not as yet adopted HIVST as a standard method. A report from New Delhi showed that HIVST was acceptable to key populations in India, which resulted in promoting plans to roll it out among these communities (71). From September 2021 to June 2022, over 93,380 HIVST kits were distributed across 14 states in India through various channels, including private practitioners, community pharmacies, and workplace and virtual models using both oral-fluid and blood-based kits. The ease of use and the effectiveness of HIVST in detecting new HIV cases underscored their potential for enhancing access to testing, encouraging preventive measures, and improving service delivery for pre-exposure prophylaxis (PrEP) (72).

Improving access to sexual and reproductive health services

Adolescents, regardless of their sexual activity or marital status, have unique sexual and reproductive health needs. A considerable number of adolescents worldwide engage in sexual activities, with frequency increasing from middle to late adolescence (73). Initiating sexual activity at an early age increases the likelihood of contracting sexually transmitted infections (STIs), including HIV and having unintended pregnancy. Thus, specific health needs of adolescents often remain unmet due to various factors such as lack of knowledge, social stigma, legal and policy barriers to accessing contraceptives and abortion services for unmarried adolescents or adolescents in general, and judgmental attitudes among healthcare providers (74). Consequently, adolescents, particularly adolescent girls, face significant challenges in accessing sexual and reproductive health information and contraceptives, which increases their vulnerability to unintended pregnancy (75).

In 2011, the World Health Organization (WHO) issued guidelines targeting adolescents from low- and middle-income countries (LMICs) to prevent early pregnancy and adverse reproductive outcomes. These guidelines focused on four major objectives: enhancing access to and use of contraception, preventing marriage before the age of 18 years, promoting awareness of the significance of early pregnancy prevention, and preventing coerced sex (76). The World Health Organization (WHO) states that access to high-quality sexual and reproductive health information and services is a fundamental right of adolescents. In recent years, the Indian government has also taken several initiatives to cater to the needs of adolescents (51).

In India, young women, particularly those living in rural areas, face significant risks and negative sexual and reproductive health (SRH) consequences, with those aged 15–24 years contributing 41 percent of total maternal deaths in the country (77). Factors such as early marriage, coupled with a lack of SRH knowledge and information and limited ability to negotiate sexual encounters, contribute to early and unprotected sex among youth (78). Furthermore, despite several policies aimed at delaying marriage, almost half of the women aged 20-24 years (47%) report getting married before reaching the legal age of marriage, which is 18 years in India. Gender norms are also one among the many reasons for females facing SRH risks, and even with time and increase in awareness, these factors have remained unaltered. The rate of sterilization among females increased from 36 percent in NFHS-4 to 38 percent in NFHS-5, whereas the rate of male sterilization remained constant at 0.3 percent over the last seven years. Research suggests that females need to take charge of their SRH in which self-care plays a crucial role.

Global media reports and research findings have brought attention to the disruption of routine reproductive health services and the limited access to essential supplies during the COVID-19 pandemic. In India, a significant portion of public health facilities were repurposed as COVID treatment centers or their focus was redirected towards providing COVID-related care (79). Consequently, women and girls, especially those in rural areas that relied heavily on the public health system, encountered significant challenges in accessing reproductive health services (80). COVID and the associated lockdown measures profoundly affected access to abortion services for women and girls. Exacerbating the already existing difficulties in accessing sexual health services, particularly by young people. Although numerous initiatives have been implemented to address adolescent sexual and reproductive health, progress in improving health outcomes among this demographic has been gradual and uneven, underscoring the need for enhancing efforts to meet the contraceptive requirements of adolescents (81).

Ensuring access to contraceptive methods, particularly for vulnerable populations and young individuals, is crucial for their wellbeing. Adolescents require accurate information and access to safe, effective, affordable, and acceptable contraceptive methods. They should have autonomy and should be empowered to safeguard themselves against STIs.

Factoring in mental health during COVID-19 pandemic and its links to sexual and reproductive health and rights

Globally, approximately 20 percent of young individuals suffer from mental disorders. Only 7.3 percent of India's massive youth population of 365 million reported mental health problems. The stigma surrounding mental health affects the help-seeking behaviors of young people. Despite the relatively low reported prevalence of mental disorders among young people in India, the country holds the unfortunate distinction of having the highest youth suicide rate globally. Suicide ranks as the leading cause of mortality among Indian youth, underscoring the gravity of the mental health challenges they faced (82)(83)(84)(85).

In rural central India, cultural and societal norms profoundly influence the sexual behaviors of adolescents. The prevailing stigma around discussions on sex makes it challenging for teenagers to speak openly on the subject. This is due to the judgmental attitudes and condemnation from the family and the wider community (86). Premarital sexual activity is deemed immoral, casting those who engage in it as promiscuous. Furthermore, entrenched gender norms dictate distinct roles and behaviors for males and females, reinforcing expectations for girls to remain passive and for boys to assert themselves. This gender dynamic results in unequal power relations with males playing a more assertive and females a more acquiescent role (87).

The COVID-19 pandemic and associated measures had a profound impact on the mental wellbeing of individuals worldwide. Adolescents and young adults experienced heightened levels of anxiety and stress due to factors such as school closures, social isolation, and domestic violence (88)(89). The pandemic also exacerbated challenges for Indian adolescents and young adults who struggled to access mental health support and counseling. With limited opportunities for social interaction and few support networks, they faced difficulties in expressing their anxiety and seeking guidance on sensitive topics such as sexual and reproductive health. Lack of access to comprehensive sexual and reproductive health services further exacerbated their mental health concerns.

Self-care guidelines increase the options for providing healthcare (5). Expansion of the scope of self-care interventions for SRHR requires an enabling environment. Without checks and balances, a dysfunctional public health system or a weakly regulated powerful private sector can result in the inappropriate use of self-care interventions (90).

Research results

The study findings are based on discussions with 17 females, including one bisexual and two HIV-positive girls, four male college graduates, and 15 female and seven male high school students. Most of the participants in the age group between 14 and 27 years were living with their families. Only a few participants, about three to four, were attending boarding school or college. Participants in our study shared their perspectives on self-care including their understanding, knowledge, and attitudes towards maintaining their health and wellbeing.

Perceptions of self-care

Data collected from high school students and college graduates across various locations indicated that these young people had different perceptions on self-care. For many, self-care involved engaging in relaxing activities and maintaining a healthy lifestyle. However, implementing these practices was a matter of individual choice. One college graduate living with HIV shared the difficulties she faced in practicing self-care despite understanding its importance. She mentioned *"Self-care is about one's health in terms of physical and mental health. But it also about using different methods to improve oneself health and wellbeing. I would say that concerning my self-care, I am not into practicing it. I know different methods of self-care. But it is very difficult for me to express my views and opinions or what I think. I don't have any friends to talk to. I'm over-reserved which makes me overthink. Physically, I'm healthy... but mentally, I feel, I am not up to the mark."*

A 26-year-old HIV positive sexually active unmarried female

For some study participants from universities and high schools, self-care primarily involved maintaining mental and emotional health. This included prioritizing mental health, engaging in yoga, ensuring inner peace, feeling happy, and making lifestyle changes. The pandemic further highlighted the importance of self-care. A 21-year-old female graduate said, *"Self-care for me is taking care of my mental and emotional wellbeing. It also has to do with our physical and mental health. I always prioritize my health. I do yoga. So, self-care for me is taking care of my mental health."* The participants stressed on the importance of regular health check-ups and advocated for self-care, particularly for the elderly. One participant shared *"Happiness is self-care to me. I have adopted boxing and a YouTube channel. I have a gym membership but I couldn't go. Regular health check-ups are necessary."*

For most of the young people, the role of education was important in promoting self-care. They believed that if they were made aware of self-care practices at a very young age, it would be easier for them to adopt self-care. Promoting healthy social norms and reducing the stigma associated with health issues were highlighted as an essential part of self-care. A 16-year-old bisexual male from high school shared *"Self-care means many things. But getting a scientific view of this would be important. A simple example of healthy social norms is handwashing. Sensitizing children through education from a young age when they are impressionable is important. It is a biological issue and should not be stigmatized."*

The COVID-19 pandemic gave a new perspective to people for practicing self-care. People adopted healthy lifestyles post-pandemic incorporating traditional Indian remedies such as *tulsi, ashwagandha,* and *turmeric* milk to their daily routine. By increasing the focus on health and hygienic practices, the pandemic further enhance self-care practices among youth.

Understanding of sexual and reproductive health among young adults

I am not aware of sexual and reproductive health. This is the first time I have heard about the term "sexual and reproductive health". I have been informed about the reproductive system and how organs work but I am not aware what maintaining reproductive health means.

    A 16-year-old sexually inactive bisexual male high school student

In order to understand sexual and reproductive health, India's young population can be grouped under different strata based on age, gender, social class, and educational background. High school students from lower economic backgrounds were likely to be from public educational institutions. The study revealed that high school students of similar age but with differences in social and educational backgrounds had varied understanding of SRH. For example, high school students from higher social classes and private educational institutions were more likely to be aware of SRH than students from public educational institutions with weaker economic and social backgrounds. One of the male participants studying at a private high school with a higher social background shared, *"I can't remember all that but I have heard of this concept. This term is not that familiar to me. No, not really. Is it if you have some kind of problem with sexual activity? Yeah, a bit. It's not too much in detail. I am not sure about many things I have heard but I guess family planners and gynecologists can help you with that."*

High school students from lower social backgrounds and public educational institutions, especially girls, mentioned that they were only aware of menstruation hygiene when asked 'What is SRH?'. They also mentioned that they were provided with sanitary pads at their schools to maintain hygiene, through government programs.

"We were taught about periods in the sixth standard at school and were asked to use sanitary napkins. I faced extreme pain and felt uneasy. But I still use them."
     A 19-year-old sexually inactive heterosexual female college graduate

Understanding of SRH changed with increasing age. This was mainly due to the change in the social circle and/or if they got involved in sexual practices. For example, young people living with HIV, married couples, and sexually active unmarried men and women had a better understanding of SRH.

"It is absolutely necessary to be aware of SRH. For the benefit of a healthy body, one should follow and utilize the practice also."

A 29-year-old sexually active heterosexual male college graduate

" SRH is extremely important because it affects other aspects of your health. For example, if you have a sexually transmitted infection, it will affect your everyday condition. I have a friend who has polycystic ovary syndrome. It affects her mood and she has to deal with the symptoms."

A 25-year-old sexually active heterosexual HIV-positive female college graduate

However, awareness about safe sexual practices was limited to knowledge of family planning. One of the male high school students from a private school said, *"SRH is to take care of yourself."*.

"My sister-in-law told me not to have sex right after the periods to avoid pregnancy. I was told not to carry heavy weights during pregnancy."

A 20-year-old married mother and high school student

It was exceptional for young people living with HIV to be aware of the use of condoms to protect against HIV.

"We should not avoid using sexual health interventions if we are going to have intercourse. Reproduction means to have a family. Nothing else. No."

A 27-year-old married female college graduate

Sources of information

The study revealed that the initial source of information about SRH typically came from schools where the reproductive system was part of the curriculum from grade five onwards. Therefore, for the high school students who were less aware of SRH, it usually depended on how openly the topic was discussed by the teacher and in which grade they received the information.

"We have learned quite a lot about it from 5th grade onwards in school. We were exposed to it"

A 16-year-old sexually inactive heterosexual female high school student

"We have a chapter in the 10th standard about sexual health, but our teachers are not open to discussing it."

A 20-year-old sexually inactive heterosexual female high school student

In high school, there was a special emphasis on providing complete information about mensuration. Their mothers were the first ones to educate young girls about it. *"We receive this education from the school. We have to take care of our sexual health and practice changing pads thrice a day. We are taught not to have junk and oily food. We are provided pads from schools through the government. If we don't get them, then our mothers buy them for us. During the pandemic, we had to buy them on our own."*

A 20-year-old sexually inactive heterosexual female college graduate

Secondary sources of information were either the internet, social media pages, TV advertisements, or NGOs. One of the females living with HIV shared her experience in getting education about sexual interventions through various events and from NGOs. *"When I was in grade 8 there was a chapter on SRHR. I got an opportunity to attend several events and lectures on the subject as they were offering these learnings on the National AIDS Control Organization (NACO) guidelines on SRHR."*

The participants mentioned accessing health-related information through Facebook and Twitter. Google was the most widely used search engine for articles on these topics. Participants mentioned reading multiple articles to access information and to make informed decisions. *"Google is the easiest to access articles on such topics. I went through at least 3-4 articles to make an informed decision. I looked for expert blogs. I have also used an application to track my monthly periods and mental health. But I prefer to visit a doctor."*

A 23-year-old unmarried bisexual post-graduate female

Study participants, including high school students, mentioned that it was easy to access information through mobile phones and the Internet. They could access information on various health topics, including sexual and reproductive health and rights. This was especially so among college graduates. However, some younger participants, particularly high school students, were limited because of their inability to access information freely due to parental controls and monitoring. They mentioned that the school-imposed restrictions on the use of mobile devices.

"My school laptops have trackers and my dad has put screen time trackers on my phone. It is difficult to have confidentiality being a teenager with Indian parents. I normally use a device which has no track history. Nothing is locked except from illegal sites. Also, one can use VPN sites to maintain privacy."

A 16-year-old male high school student

Our study revealed that young people frequently accessed the internet to get answers to health-related queries. However, for high school students, particularly those from better economic backgrounds, having easy access to the internet and mobile phones did not necessarily translate into a strong curiosity. Their curiosity tended to be limited to specific terms rather than to seeking comprehensive knowledge through self-directed learning. *"Most of my knowledge is from the internet and from school and peers. If I want to know about a specific thing, I go directly to Google. In school, I can ask doctors, experts, and therapists. I don't really fact check as I don't think too much about it in my day-to-day life. It's not my priority to fact check. But when it is talked about at a later stage is when I actually search for things. I normally go to Wikipedia to search about bodily functions."*

A 16-year-old sexually inactive heterosexual male high school student

A general search on the Internet was their first step. This was usually followed by cross verifying the information sources or relying on trusted health organizations to verify the accuracy of the information. A 16-year-old high school student shared *"Google is my first go to. In terms of the sources on google itself I would go for WHO and if I am looking for experiences, I go to Quora".*

"If I see something on social media, I try to find out who is saying it, whether it's a random person, a professional, or a person who experienced it. Sometimes, I Google it and look for credible pages like healthline, scholar.com, and peer-reviewed articles. I look for some links over and above other links."

A 25-year-old sexually active unmarried post-graduate female

College graduates also mentioned the importance of peer-reviewed articles and authoritative health websites and centers. A bisexual female said, *"For the most part, I look through peer-reviewed articles and take them at face value and trust what they say. Also, I would probably talk to a friend who is knowledgeable in this field. I used to do a random search. After they do it for 3-4 times, you automatically look for WebMD and Mayo Clinic which are more trustworthy."*

"Not all the information we see online is correct. I cross-checked it with the National AIDS Control Organization (NACO) website and I came to know about antiretroviral therapy (ART) centers through this website."

A 27-year-old heterosexual married male living with HIV

In spite of easy accessibility, young college graduates, especially married couples or people living with certain health conditions, showed a preference for consulting doctors if online solutions did not suffice for self-treatment. A 25-year-old married female mentioned, *"I look online for remedies. If I do not find a proper solution, I consult a doctor. It depends on the health issue I am facing."*

A college graduate living with HIV, who worked at an ART center, shared his experience with the role of ART centers and consultation with health authorities. He specifically mentioned that they provided information on HIV. He also discussed the role of ART centers during the COVID-19 pandemic. *"One HIV positive patient came to me and told me that some ayurvedic medicine can cure HIV and he started taking medicines after searching it online. So, I asked him to take the proper medicine."*

Self-care interventions for sexual and reproductive health and rights

The study revealed that there was a strong reliance on school education for developing an understanding, attitudes, and practices related to self-care interventions for SRH. Interestingly, in India, although most young people lived with their parents, they did not depend on families to educate teenagers about SRH. There was a lot of hesitation in talking about SRH.

"Yeah, my school keeps discussing it. We had a few sessions at my previous school and now we have more detailed discussions on contraceptives, abstinence, and STIs in this school. I got to know about masturbation first from friends but yeah that's how I learned about it. But then we had a few sessions from grade six about gender identity and gender awareness. In grade 10, we had weekly sessions on this. I learnt about how the body changes and how to prevent getting STDs were mainly through schools, friends, and external sessions."

A 16-year-old sexually inactive heterosexual male high school student

Our study indicated that the young people's self-education efforts were primarily driven by curiosity and interest. Limited factors were mentioned regarding knowledge acquisition, especially by sexually inactive high school students between 15 and 19 years of age. A 17-year-old high school girl said, *"We never think about sex in this way"*. Youth were aware of contraceptives like male condoms, female condoms, birth control pills, self-testing kits like pregnancy test kits and self-management interventions like abortion pills. But they lacked knowledge about self-injectable contraceptives and contraceptive vaginal rings. One of the high school students said, *"I am aware about condoms and birth control pills (after sex maybe). I am not aware of it in detail."*

Young girls, including high school students and college graduates, who shared their understanding of sexual health, said that they practiced menstrual hygiene. They felt that they had been made aware of all the necessary precautions for maintaining healthy behaviors during menstruation. High school girls preferred using pads while college graduates were more open to using other options like tampons and menstrual cups.

"I have irregular periods, and whenever it happens, it lasts for 15 days, which causes rashes and irritation. I am taking medicine."
A 17-year-old sexually inactive heterosexual high school female

"I use sanitary napkins. I've tried using a menstrual cup."
A 25-year-old sexually active heterosexual college graduate female

Sexually active youth were aware of lubricants for sexual pleasure, but they tended to have a casual attitude toward using self-care interventions for sexual health. They preferred using contraceptives. They relied primarily on male condoms, followed by birth control pills. Their knowledge and practice of using long-term birth control methods was limited (or entirely absent). This was also true for married couples. *"There are different ones for males and females. For females, I'm aware of Copper T which is kind of like a T that covers your fallopian tubes. My partner uses a condom, I don't use anything."*
A 25-year-old sexually active heterosexual female college graduate

One of the male college graduates admitted to having had four relationships in the past. He was made aware of contraceptive methods at a very young age by one of his family members. However, these young people did not use condoms. They opted for over-the-counter emergency contraceptives. Even though married girls were aware of birth control options, mostly relied on condoms that were used by their partners. One of the married female graduates said, *"We are using condoms to avoid getting pregnant. I avoid taking pills because I feel they're harmful. We do sometimes follow traditional practices. If I'm about to have my period, we have intercourse without using the condom."*

"I believe I have some knowledge about SRH. But I have not availed of any services as my partner is a female."

A 23-year-old sexually active bisexual college graduate female

Young bisexuals and people living with HIV had a good understanding of self-care interventions. They practiced healthy sexual behaviors while engaging in sexual activities by using condoms. One of the married females living with HIV said, *"We use condoms to prevent HIV. Our sexual and reproductive health is of utmost priority."* People living with HIV were also more cautious about their sexual lives and went for health checkups regularly.

"I recently shifted to India so I haven't gone to any health facility. But when I was in Nepal, I used to go to the family planning organization and they did periodic checkups. It is very important. In our relationship, this is important because my partner is HIV positive, and I am HIV negative. It is important for us to know about SRH because there may be unsafe sex or other risky behaviors that we should not do to prevent STDs and unwanted pregnancy. We need to take precautions and we need to have the right information."

A 26-year-old heterosexual female living with HIV

Abortion

"I definitely feel that it's every woman's choice. I am unmarried, and there are societal issues. If I get pregnant without getting married, it will be hell for my family. It is not acceptable. It's a choice that lies with the family and with women. My parents have 16 siblings. Family planning was not a concept at that time. By 25 or 28, you should have your first kid, and by 32, the second one."

A 24-year-old sexually active heterosexual college graduate female

Our study highlighted the complex reality of abortion in India. Despite its legality, a strong stigma surrounds abortion. Young people are hesitant to discuss it openly. One sexually active male said, *"I don't feel comfortable talking about my sexual health. Depending on the severity, I will consult the doctor."* Most of the young married couples viewed abortion from a family planning perspective only. However, abortion is legal, young married couples felt more comfortable talking about it. They said that it was a personal choice and a health concern for women to prevent pregnancy.

"Abortion is practiced to save the life of the mother. Also, it's a personal choice that people make. Sometimes the mother is not fully capable of taking care of the child, but sometimes that's for the good."
A 21-year-old sexually inactive heterosexual college graduate female

High school students shared that they had little to no awareness of abortion. A high school boy said, *"I know there are some techniques of abortion, but I don't know exactly how they work."*

Our study also showed that young people were not aware of self-testing and self-sampling for HIV, STIs, and HPV. They perceived these conditions to be serious health concerns and preferred to consult a doctor rather than adopt self-care through self-testing.

"As soon as you talk about STIs and HIV, it becomes a serious condition to deal with; I would not depend on self-care for it but would go to the doctor."
A 25-year-old sexually active heterosexual college graduate female

Gender roles

Our study showed that irrespective of their gender, young people did not typically include financial and family issues in decision-making. With age, they gradually became more involved in decision-making. When asked about who makes financial decisions in the families, young people between the ages of 15 and 19 said, *"Parents make this decision."* or *"When there is a large payment, I am told about it so that I can learn to make decisions later in my life."* Young people aged 20 years and above said they were informed about major decisions. If they contributed financially, they had more of a say. Young married girls said they were more often consulted by their partners than their parents, *"I don't think my family had much to say, but with my partner, yes."* High school students discussed personal health decisions with their mothers. However, none of the high school students who were sexually inactive discussed matters related to sexual health. College graduates, on the other hand, made their own sexual health decisions. They usually went to healthcare providers with a partner or a friend for support.

"Yes, we are equally involved in the decision. No, we do not take family members to any health facility or take permission from them. But yes, we usually inform them."

A 24-year-old sexually active female living with HIV

The study revealed that young high school students from socially advantaged backgrounds were generally allowed to go out with parental supervision, regardless of gender. However, for those from less economically advantaged backgrounds, girls had fewer opportunities to go out compared to boys. College graduates, particularly those living independently, enjoyed greater freedom to go out as long as they avoided alcohol and substance abuse. However, even for college girls living with their families, going out late at night was restricted.

"When I was young, it was not that usual. It changed during college. I do expect resistance when I ask to travel for 3-4 days, but there is quite a resistance to this. If there is a requirement, then yes. Only if there is a particular need."

A 23-year-old sexually inactive bisexual college graduate female

"I am allowed to go out very minimally. It has opened up post the pandemic. My parents prefer that some adults should accompany me. But on the other hand, for some activities, they completely trust me. They are completely confident now. But some ground rules are set. If there are no adults, I have to be back home by 8 or 8.30 pm IST."

A 16-year-old sexually inactive bisexual high school male

Young girls mentioned facing sexual and physical abuse while growing up. *"We don't usually talk about abuse. You see physical abuse when you are a child. Talking about sexual abuse, I have been groped in buses. People poking and masturbating, looking at you. Yes, abuse was there. There was a lot of mental abuse by body shaming."*

A 23-year-old sexually active bisexual college graduate female

The study revealed that young people, in general, lacked confidence in their ability to perform tasks effectively or achieve their goals. However, regarding their sexual health, opinions were more polarized with strong agreements and disagreements.

The research indicated that sexually active young people exhibited less consensus on statements like *"it is easy to talk about sex with a partner"* and *"you can tell your partner if you do not want to have sex."* This was particularly true for young unmarried girls who were sexually active. These girls, especially those in new relationships, admitted feeling pressured to conform to certain expectations. They felt that they had no say during sex. But inspite of feeling a certain way while having sex, young girls mentioned getting complete support in sexual matters from their partners.

"My partner also recognizes that sexual and reproductive health is really important. We talk about it and take enough precautions and care to ensure that my health is at its best."

A 25-year-old sexually active female living with HIV

Young married girls were comfortable in sharing their sexual experiences and mentioned getting full support from their male partners in pregnancy-related matters. They strongly disagreed with the statement *"I feel pressure to be a certain way during sex"*. *"My husband sometimes uses condoms. I was told that one should not have sex during periods as it can cause swelling and during pregnancy as it can harm the baby. My husband always accompanies me to the hospital. I only went there for tests during the 8th and 9th month of my pregnancy."*

A 20-year-old married college graduate female

Some of the young girls openly shared their thoughts about their struggles. One of them said, *"Girls don't know how to say no. They don't know about their right to decide when to have children. Sexual activities are also not discussed in public. It is one aspect of our life where we should be allowed to make decisions related to it."*

A young girl shared that her parents' decisions regarding her marriage conflicted with her own desires. *"My parents say the earlier you get married, the better it is. It is always like what the family wants and not what we want for ourselves."* However, she hoped that things would change with time, believing today's society is different from the one their mothers dealt with in their youth. "Suppose I want to have a kid or not; that definition has changed with surrogacy, and this is so important. *My mother had a career and she had kids because her family wanted that. Her whole life was around her kids. She is a home-maker now. Abortion is every woman's choice. People are talking about it with a broad mind. Society wants women to be taken care of by their husbands. It's not about having a kid; it's about my body. It changes everything— my finances and everything. My partner may have a say in it but ultimately it's a woman's choice"*

A 24-year-old sexually active heterosexual female college graduate

Self-care and the COVID-19 factor

Change in routine during the pandemic

The participants said that there were significant changes in their daily routines, lifestyles, physical activities, and self-care practices during the COVID-19 pandemic. Disruptions caused by lockdowns and social distancing measures led to modifications in how they managed their time, their health, and their social interactions.

A 21-year-old female college graduate shared her routine, mentioning, *"I get up early and exercise. Then, I attend online lectures and engage in several things. I like to keep myself busy. When there was no pandemic, I could go out easily. I missed this during the pandemic. I missed talking to my friends. I talked to them online only."*

"Before the pandemic, I had been taking care of myself, but during the pandemic, my daily routine was affected. I used to walk and take 12 rounds of the campus. Coming back home, it was not the same lifestyle."

A 23-year-old sexually actively unmarried female bisexual

Participants also shared that their was increased dependence on social media during the pandemic. It became an important tool to stay connected and to share information with peers. An unmarried girl said *"During the pandemic we had greater dependence on social media. There was a group for COVID information in our college. They tried to support people. We brought an oximeter and a steamer."*

The pandemic highlighted the adaptability of young people in managing their self-care practices. They adjusted their routines and were more on social media for interaction with friends and family and for getting health information. Despite this, they faced challenges in maintaining regular physical activity. They also had to reduce in-person socialization.

Challenges faced by young people with respect to sexual and reproductive health during COVID-19 pandemic

Participants discussed issues faced in accessing health services during the pandemic. They highlighted problems regarding the implementation of services by the Indian government. One of the participants who was 26-years-old, said *"Planning is there by the government but execution is lacking. I believe Mohalla Clinics should be more easily accessible to the people."* Participants mentioned that there were gaps in policy planning and in program implementation which hindered service delivery.

"My mother faced deoxygenation and was stigmatized to tell anyone. We were scared that they would close our street. It was a challenge to take her to the hospital and to get her medicine."

A sexually inactive, unmarried female

Participants shared that in India, they cannot watch TV on sexual life in front of their parents. They mentioned facing stigma within their families. It was inconvenient to discuss sexual health related matters. Most female participants shared their ideas about reproductive health with their mothers.

" Because of my HIV status, people did not accept us and started to discriminate. My aunt helped us. In 2007, when my father expired, I came to know that I am HIV positive. My younger brother also tested positive and he started his medication in 2010."

A 24-years-old HIV positive married female

Participants also mentioned that they had difficulties in accessing health services during the second wave of the pandemic.

"For many months, I couldn't access a doctor because of the rules and the severity of the second wave. However, this situation lasted only for a few months. After that, the services bounced back pretty quickly.

A 16-years-old bisexual male high school student

The participants said that the COVID-19 pandemic significantly impacted their family's financial stability. It affected their livelihoods and long-term financial stability. A 23-year-old unmarried bisexual girl said, *"My father had retired, so there was a sudden halt in the family's monthly income. I was living in a hostel where monthly expenses needed to be covered. Upon my return from Hyderabad, I didn't have any money, which was not the case earlier. I faced a lot of problems which affected my freedom. Financial decisions were delayed and one needed to think before buying anything."*

During the pandemic, many families struggled to manage their finances without regular income. Several young people from lower socioeconomic backgrounds had parents who relied on daily income, and some had no work during the pandemic.

"My parents had no work for three months. Finances were affected and we had no money to survive. The Kejriwal government provided free rations, electricity, water, and transportation which somehow helped us to survive during the pandemic."

A 14-year-old female from urban slum from India

Mental health support from social and governmental networks

Participants highlighted the importance of positive thinking and regular discussion with peers for their mental wellbeing. They said that social disconnect led to depression and suicidal thoughts. A female participant mentioned, *"Positive thinking, meeting, and discussing things is necessary. Correct information is important. Depression disconnects people and it is very risky. A person may commit suicide. Expressing feelings is very important."*

A 26-year-old unmarried, active heterosexual female living with HIV said that her struggle for her illness was exacerbated by depression. She shared, *"I was diagnosed with depression in 2011. I developed fibromyalgia in 2015. I experienced intense pain in the joints and these symptoms led to paralysis. I was bedridden. My illness was a result of a long mental issue. My condition was very poor. I had feelings of loneliness and suffered from lack of sleep."*

The participants said that they experienced severe mental health issues for the first time during the pandemic. They relied on social interactions to cope. People with existing mental health issues suffered prolonged crises.

"The routine affected my lifestyle and my mental health. I couldn't share this with my friends. The monotonous routine affected me badly. I experienced anxiety issues after six months of the lockdown. I consulted a doctor friend and she advised me to think about avoiding loneliness. Don't keep things inside. She said that expression is necessary, and it worked."

A 26-years-old sexually active unmarried male

"Fortunately, I've never faced severe mental health issues like depression and anxiety. I have friends who have dealt with this. I experienced this for the first time during the pandemic."

A 25-year-old sexually active female post-graduate student

Participants underscored the need for accessible mental health resources, the importance of maintaining social connections, and the role of government in providing healthcare services for sustaining mental wellbeing during the crisis. They emphasized the role of peer support and communities in providing an understanding environment. They emphasized that families and friends were an important support system for managing the mental health challenges they faced. A 23-year-old bisexual female said, *"I first reached out to my friends with whom I felt very comfortable talking. They helped me to reach out to external support. During the peak of the pandemic, isolation was a huge problem. At this point, I came across an Instagram profile for a mental health peer group, and I joined it. I could talk about my problems there. You find people, pages, and other things that help you find a safe space to get help, and you feel a little better. I stayed away from the more scientific pages. The grief and the hurt were traumatic. It saddened me. I didn't have the space to face this."*

The participants described how the role of ASHA workers had been instrumental in providing information on self-care and vaccination. Free rations by the government were a significant support to many families. However, not all the needy could access them, which was very critical, especially for the daily wage workers. People from the backward classes were dismissive of precautions, considering it a matter of fate. A 23-year-old bisexual female college graduate said, *"A group of ASHA workers was very active in providing information on vaccination. The government provided vaccines for free. Free rations were provided for at least 1.5 years. We had to go to the ration shops to get rations."*

Participants highlighted how social networks played a significant role in providing health services and filled the gaps left by the government.

"Social networks were a major help during the pandemic. Oxygen cylinders, hospital beds, and other important things were arranged through these networks. I went for plasma donation and saw a few things that were difficult to see. There was a lack of support from the government.

A 26-years-old sexually active male

Motivation for the uptake of self-care interventions

Most participants said that of the over-the-counter contraceptives, condom was the best method. They also discussed their preference for birth control pills. However, most male participants said that *"It should be the woman's decision whether to use it or not."* The major motivating factor for using contraceptives was its effectiveness and ease of use.

"I think it also depends on my partner's choice, as sex involves two partners." According to the participants, the decision to use emergency contraception and to use lubricants was influenced by the quality of the product and the preference of both partners involved. Participants acknowledged that there should be shared responsibility in taking sexual health decisions. Their strong inclination was to use emergency contraception to maintain privacy. The participants also underscored the importance of consulting healthcare professionals for making informed decisions.

Discussion

India currently has its largest ever youth population. According to the United Nations Fund for Population Activities (UNFPA) projections, India will continue to have one of the youngest populations in the world till 2030 (91). India's youth face several developmental challenges. They need access to education, gainful employment, gender equality, and youth-friendly health services. Most of these challenges are associated with sexual and reproductive health concerns. There is, therefore, a need to invest in the youth of India with a special concern for these factors to transform the social and economic nature of the country. Our research study reflected on some of these factors. The study included young populations from the various regions of the country representing different socioeconomic backgrounds and different levels of education. Our research highlighted that there is a significant gap in the understanding of SRH by young people in India. Factors such as socioeconomic status, access to education, age, and marital/sexual health status significantly influence their understanding of SRH concepts. The study also shed light on the knowledge, attitudes, and practices related to self-care interventions for SRH in young people. It showed that there was an interplay of factors that influenced how young people perceive and engage in self-care. These include the role of education, family dynamics, societal norms, and access to information.

The research indicated that there is limited family involvement in SRH education of young people. There is hesitation and discomfort in discussing these topics at home and, in general, within society. Research by Byers et al. indicates that parents avoid discussing sexual topics due to discomfort, embarrassment, lack of knowledge, fear of encouraging early sexual activity, and assumptions that adolescents receive information from schools and the media (92). There is a disparity in SRH knowledge among students from lower social and educational backgrounds. Students from lower economic backgrounds, especially those in public institutions, are aware of menstrual hygiene but have very limited knowledge on SRH.

India has made much progress in improving the sexual and reproductive health of women and young people by implementing special programs focused on youth. Examples are the National Family Planning Programme, focusing on expanding the contraceptive method mix, and the *Rashtriya Kishor Swasthya Karyakram*, which prioritizes healthy development during adolescence (39)). Our study indicated that programs were successful by highlighting the level of awareness regarding SRH among young people. It also highlighted that there were critical gaps in addressing adolescent sexual and reproductive health needs. Many young people were left with no option but to self-educate about SRH. Young people's self-educational efforts are largely driven by curiosity and interest, particularly for sexually inactive high school youth who have a superficial understanding of contraceptives. Their knowledge of self-injectables, contraceptives, self-testing, self-sampling, and self-management is either limited or totally missing. Young people believe that HIV, STIs, and HPV are serious health issues that require professional medical consultation rather than problems that can be addressed by self-care interventions.

UNICEF statistics (2003–2008) show only 20 percent of Indian adolescent girls have comprehensive HIV/AIDS knowledge. Awareness is higher in urban areas and among males. Awareness correlates with education levels (14). Kumar et al. (2012) found that there were no effective sources of SRH information despite existing AIDS education programs in schools (14). These findings underscore the need for providing targeted interventions and more comprehensive education in public schools.

India's abortion law is perceived to be liberal. But societal attitudes and medical practitioners' moral perspectives complicate women's experiences of seeking abortion services as stated by the National Law School, 2021 (93). This is also supported by our research study, which indicates that young people view abortion from a family planning perspective, especially married women who consider it as a personal choice and health concern. Abortion remains a stigmatized and sensitive topic in society despite its legality in

India. Consequently, people feel uncomfortable talking about it openly.

Our research suggests that the understanding of SRH evolves with age and life experience. Individuals living with HIV, married couples, and sexually active young people have a better understanding compared to their younger and sexually inactive counterparts. Youth are cautious about self-care interventions. They regularly consult health professionals and undergo health checkups. These findings underscore the importance of integrating SRH education into mainstream healthcare programs. The evolving needs of young people should be addressed. Many young people above 20 years of age equate SRH with family planning and menstrual hygiene and have a casual attitude towards sex. While young people are aware of lubricants and basic contraceptives, their knowledge of long-term birth control methods is limited. The NFHS-5 report stated that, on average, women reported their first sexual intercourse at a younger age than men as they got married much earlier than men. Ten percent of women were sexually active at the age of 15. Only one percent of men were sexually active at that age. Despite early sexual debut, women's knowledge of contraception was lower than that of men. These findings underscore the importance of SRH education at the high school level (94).

Our study underscored the importance of gender and highlighted how age, gender, and socioeconomic background influenced young people's participation in family, financial, and personal health decisions. Adolescents primarily saw their parents making financial decisions. They were occasionally informed about major purchases but only for their learning experience. However, young college graduates were more involved in decision-making. There was a gradual shift towards greater autonomy as young people aged. Young, married girls started feeling more included in decision-making after marriage with their partners/husbands than with their parents. Our study also highlighted that decision-making in young adults and college graduates was limited to their health. There were notable differences based on gender and socioeconomic status. Males had more freedom than females. There were ongoing challenges for young women in navigating societal and familial expectations.

Our study underscored that young people who were HIV positive had a better understanding of SRH. This indicates that HIV awareness programs in India are successful in generating awareness. Similar programs should be implemented to generate a better understanding of SRH interventions.

The high burden of mental health disorders among adolescents to identify effective interventions is planned to address this problem. There is emerging evidence from high-income countries that interventions in different settings and life domains can contribute to good mental health in adolescents (95). Unfortunately, there is a dearth of such mental health interventions in India and even fewer that have been evaluated (96).

Our research underscored that the young population above the age of 15 in India required more educational programs as education plays a crucial role in shaping one's perceptions of self-care. It is important to introduce topics such as self-care and sexual and reproductive health at a young age in order to normalize healthy social norms and reduce stigma.

Concluding comments

The study underscores the complex landscape of SRH understanding among young people in India. It reveals significant gaps in SRH knowledge, particularly among young people from lower socioeconomic backgrounds and public schools. There is limited family involvement. There is a reliance on schools for providing young people with SRH information. Various societal norms shape young people's understanding of sexual matters. Our study highlights the preferences among youth in accessing and utilizing health information. It emphasizes the need for reliable sources of information. It also highlights young people's preference for in-person medical consultation over online resources.

Comprehensive SRH education programs should be implemented to address the needs of young people. Normalizing discussions on SRH can help to reduce stigma and, thereby, enhance awareness among people. It is important to integrate SRH education within mainstream educational systems. Sex education should be tailored to the needs of young people in different age groups and from various socioeconomic backgrounds.

There is a serious paucity of research on self-care among young people globally and in India. Therefore, it is recommended that more research be undertaken on this topic.

Acknowledgments

The authors thank Manish Gupta, a Youth Mentor at the POP Movement, for helping them reach the targeted groups included in the study. We appreciate his support for this research endeavor.

References

1. Narasimhan M, Hargreaves JR, Logie CH, Abdool-Karim Q, Aujla M, Hopkins J, et al. Self-care interventions for women's health and well-being. Nature Medicine. 2024 Mar; 30(3): 660–669. https://www.nature.com/articles/s41591-024-02844-8

2. Tran N T, Tappis H, Moon P, Christofield M & Dawson A. Self-Care for sexual and reproductive health in humanitarian and fragile settings. Conflict and Health 15. 2021 Apr 07; 22(2021). https://conflictandhealth.biomedcentral.com/articles/10.1186/s13031-021-00358-5#citeas

3. Narasimhan M, Iongh A de, Askew I, Simpson PJ. It's time to recognise self care as an integral component of health systems. British Medical Journal. 2019 Apr 1; 365: l403. https://www.bmj.com/content/365/bmj.l403

4. Mathias E.G, D'souza A & Prabhu. Self-medication practices among the adolescent population of South Karnataka, India. Journal of Environmental and Public Health - Wiley Online Library. 2020 Sep 7; 2020(1). https://online

library.wiley.com/doi/10.1155/2020/9021819

5. Narasimhan M, Logie C.H, Hargreaves J, Janssens W, Aujla M, Steyn P, Sijpt E.V.D & Hardon A. Self-care interventions for advancing sexual and reproductive health and rights – implementation considerations. Journal of Global Health Reports. 2023 Aug 21; 7. https://www.joghr.org/article/84086-self-care-interventions-for-advancing-sexual-and-reproductive-health-and-rights-implementation-considerations

6. Khanna R, Sheth M, Talati P, Damor K & Chauhan B. Social and economic marginalisation and sexual and reproductive health and rights of urban poor young women: a qualitative study from Vadodara, Gujarat, India. Sexual and Reproductive Health Matters; 29(2): 2059898. https://www.ncbi.nlm.nih.gov/pmc/articles/PMC9067967/

7. Population Foundation of India. Comprehensive sexuality education in India: A review of government and civil society-led curricula and strategies. Population Foundation of India. 2022 Apr. https://www.populationfoundation.in/wp-content/uploads/2022/07/A-review-of-government-and-civil-society-led-CSE-curricula-and-strategies-in-India-1.pdf

8. Shukla R.T. Issues related to adolescent sexuality and role of socio-cultural factors in sexual behaviors among adolescents in India. All India Institute of Medi. 2016 Dec. https://www.researchgate.net/publication/314257727_Issues_Related_to_Adolescent_Sexuality_and_Role_of_Socio-cultural_Factors_in_Sexual_Behaviors_among_Adolescents_in_India

9. Hakim N. Sources of information and norms regarding sexual issues among Indian male young adults. University of Michigan. 2012. https://deepblue.lib.umich.edu/bitstream/handle/2027.42/91874/nhhakim.pdf

10. Ubale PD, Sekher TV. Risky Sexual Behaviors Among Unmarried Youth in India: Evidences from National Family Health Survey, 2019–21. In: Deb S, Deb S, editors. Handbook of Youth Development. Singapore: Springer Nature Singapore; 2023. 413–439. https://link.springer.com/10.1007/978-981-99-4969-4_24

11. Kundu T & Bhattacharya P. Sex in India: What data shows. mint. 2018 May 25. https://www.livemint.com/Politics/RC0cvSgItInzrPBjAZ3f2L/Sex-in-India-What-data-shows.html

12. Salam RA, Faqqah A, Sajjad N, Lassi ZS, Das JK, Kaufman M, et al. Improving Adolescent Sexual and Reproductive Health: A Systematic Review of Potential Interventions. Journal of Adolescent Health. 2016 Oct; 59: 11–28. https://www.ncbi.nlm.nih.gov/pmc/articles/PMC5026684/

13. Burke HM, Ridgeway K, Murray K, Mickler A, Thomas R & Williams K. Reproductive empowerment and contraceptive self-care: a systematic review. Sexual and Reproductive Health Matters 2022 Jul 27; 29(3): 2090057. https://www.ncbi.nlm.nih.gov/pmc/articles/PMC9336472/

14. Mukhopadhyay S & Mishra S.K. Knowledge and practices about sexual health and its socioeconomic correlates among adolescent girls in Sikkim, India. Sage Journals. 2021 Apr 11; 21(1). https://journals.sagepub.com/doi/abs/10.1177/0972558X211001156?journalCode=oana#bibr30-0972558X211001156

15. Vanestanagh AK, Farshbaf-Khalili A, Esmaeilpour K, Jafarabadi MA, & Jahdi NS. Effect of smartphone-based education on knowledge and self-care of reproductive health in married students. Journal of Education and Health Promotion. 2021 Mar 31; 10: 89. https://www.ncbi.nlm.nih.gov/pmc/articles/PMC8150067/

16. Self-care Trailblazer Group. Self-Care: For youth, by youth. PSI. 2021 May 21. https://www.psi.org/project/self-care/self-care-for-youth-by-youth/

17. Boler T & Jellema A. Deadly inertia: cross-country study of educational responses to HIV/AIDS. Child Rights International Network. 2005 Nov. https://archive.crin.org/en/library/publications/deadly-inertia-cross-country-study-educational-responses-hiv/aids.html

18. Lal P, Nath A, Badhan S & Ingle GK. A Study of Awareness about HIV/AIDS Among Senior Secondary School Children of Delhi. Indian Journal of Community Medicine: Official Publication of Indian Association of Preventive & Social Medicine. 2008 Jul; 33(3): 190–192. https://www.ncbi.nlm.nih.gov/pmc/articles/PMC2763684/

19. Bertrand JT & Anhang R. The effectiveness of mass media in changing HIV/AIDS-related behaviour among young people in developing countries. World Health Organization of Technical Report Series. 2006; 938: 205–241;

discussion 317-341. https://pubmed.ncbi.nlm.nih.gov/16921921/

20. The Hindu Bureau. Increase in minimum age of marriage for women to 21 years two years after Bill is notified: Centre.The Hindu. 2023 Mar 16. https://www.thehindu.com/news/national/increase-in-minimum-age-of-marriage-for-women-to-21-years-two-years-after-bill-is-notified-centre/article66622738.ece

21. World Population Review. Age of consent by country 2024. World Population Review. https://worldpopulationreview.com/country-rankings/age-of-consent-by-country

22. Girls Not Brides. The impact of age of marriage and sexual consent laws on child marriage and girls' rights. Girls Not Brides. 2024 Feb 27. https://www.girlsnotbrides.org/learning-resources/events/impact-age-of-marriage-sexual-consent-laws-child-marriage-girls-rights/

23. Chakrabarty S. Fault lines emerge in debate over age of consent and marriage for women. The Hindu. 2023 Jul 31. https://www.thehindu.com/news/national/fault-lines-emerge-in-debate-over-age-of-consent-and-marriage-for-women/article67135808.ece

24. Optimize IAS. Age of consent in India - Optimize IAS. 2023 Feb 8. https://optimizeias.com/age-of-consent-in-india/

25. Ramteke RU, Makade JG & Bandre GR. Adolescent sexual behavior in rural central India: Challenges and interventions. Cureus. 2023 Nov; 15(11): 49761. https://www.ncbi.nlm.nih.gov/pmc/articles/PMC10758265/

26. Sunitha S & Gururaj G. Health behaviours & problems among young people in India: Cause for concern & call for action. Indian Journal of Medical Research. 2014 Aug; 140(2): 185–208. https://www.ncbi.nlm.nih.gov/pmc/articles/PMC4216492/

27. Chandra R, Paul P & Srivastava S. Prevalence and predictors of risky sexual behavior among young men in India: Evidence from national family health survey. International Journal of Sexual Health: Official Journal of World Association of Sexual Health. 2024; 36(1): 32–45. https://pubmed.ncbi.nlm.nih.gov/38600902/

28. Kenndy E. Sexual and reproductive health of unmarried young people in Asia and the Pacific: Review of knowledge, behaviours, and outcomes. United

Nations Population Fund. 2015. https://asiapacific.unfpa.org/sites/default/files/pub-pdf/SRH%20of%20Ummarried%20Young%20People%20in%20Asia%20Pacific.pdf

29. International Institute for Population Sciences. National family health survey (NFHS-4). Ministry of Health and Family Welfare. 2017 Dec. https://dhsprogram.com/pubs/pdf/FR339/FR339.pdf

30. Stillman, Frost J.J, Sahoo H, Alagarajan M, Sundaram A, Kalyanwala S & Ball H. Abortion and unintended pregnancy in six Indian states: Findings and implications for policies and programs. Guttmacher Institute. 2018 Nov. https://www.guttmacher.org/report/abortion-unintended-pregnancy-six-states-india

31. Sharma H & Singh SK. The burden of unintended pregnancies among Indian adolescent girls in Bihar and Uttar Pradesh: findings from the UDAYA survey (2015–16 & 2018–19). Archives of Public Health. 2023 Apr 27; 81(1): 75. https://doi.org/10.1186/s13690-023-01077-4

32. Peach E, Morgan C, Scoullar M.J.L. Fowkes F.J.I., Kennedy E, Melepia P et al. Risk factors and knowledge associated with high unintended pregnancy rates and low family planning use among pregnant women in Papua New Guinea. Scientific Reports. 2021 Jan 31. https://www.nature.com/articles/s41598-020-79103-6

33. Chandra-Mouli V, McCarraher DR, Phillips SJ, Williamson NE & Hainsworth G. Contraception for adolescents in low- and middle-income countries: needs, barriers, and access. Reproductive Health. 2014 Jan 2; 11(1): 1. https://pubmed.ncbi.nlm.nih.gov/24383405/

34. Sarkar A, Chandra-Mouli V, Jain K, Behera J, Mishra SK & Mehra S. Community based reproductive health interventions for young married couples in resource-constrained settings: a systematic review. BioMed Central Public Health. 2015 Oct 9; 15: 1037. https://pubmed.ncbi.nlm.nih.gov/26452750/

35. Singh S, Shekhar C, Acharya R, Moore AM, Stillman M, Pradhan MR, et al. The incidence of abortion and unintended pregnancy in India, 2015. Lancet of Global Health. 2018 Jan; 6(1): 111–120. https://pubmed.ncbi.nlm.nih.gov/29241602/

36. Klima CS. Unintended pregnancy. Consequences and solutions for a worldwide problem. Journal of Nurse-Midwifery. 1998; 43(6): 483–491. https://pubmed.ncbi.nlm.nih.gov/9871381/

37. Murro R, Chawla R, Pyne S, Venkatesh S & Sully EA. Adding It Up: Investing in the Sexual and Reproductive Health of Adolescents in India. Guttmacher Institute. 2023 Mar 31. https://www.guttmacher.org/report/adding-it-up-investing-in-sexual-reproductive-health-adolescents-india

38. P.M A. Concerns around abortion in India differ from those in the West. Frontline. 2022 Oct 20. https://frontline.thehindu.com/columns/concerns-around-abortion-in-india-differ-from-those-in-the-west/article66000417.ece

39. Murro R, Chawla R, Pyne S, Venkatesh S & Sully EA. Adding it up: Investing in the sexual and reproductive health of adolescents in India. Guttmacher. 2021 Mar 31. https://www.guttmacher.org/report/adding-it-up-investing-in-sexual-reproductive-health-adolescents-india

40. Chakraborty R. How the abortion pill Mifepristone is being misused and sending young women to the ER. Used right, it's safe. The Indian Express. 2023 Apr 18. https://indianexpress.com/article/health-wellness/abortion-pill-mifepristone-misused-sending-young-women-er-8562847/

41. Peshawaria T. Docs worried about rising teen pregnancy, self-abortion in Gurgaon. Times of India. 2013 Jul 24. https://timesofindia.indiatimes.com/life-style/spotlight/docs-worried-about-rising-teen-pregnancy-self-abortion-in-gurgaon/articleshow/21274442.cms?utm_source=contentofinterest&utm_medium=text&utm_campaign=cppst

42. Vardaan Hospital. Busting myths on abortion pills. Vardaan Hospital. https://www.vardaan.net/busting-myths-on-abortion-pills

43. Jejeebhoy SJ, Kalyanwala S, Zavier AJF, Kumar R & Jha N. Experience seeking abortion among unmarried young women in Bihar and Jharkhand, India: delays and disadvantages. Reproductive Health Matters. 2010 May; 18(35): 163–174. https://pubmed.ncbi.nlm.nih.gov/20541095/

44. Aras RY, Pai NP & Jain SG. Termination of pregnancy in adolescents. Journal of Postgraduate Medicine. 1987 Jul; 33(3): 120–124. https://pubmed.ncbi.nlm.nih.gov/3430397/

45. Kalyanwala S, Zavier AJF, Jejeebhoy S & Kumar R. Abortion experiences of unmarried young women in India: evidence from a facility-based study in Bihar and Jharkhand. International Perspective on Sexual and Reproductive Health. 2010 Jun; 36(2): 62–71. https://pubmed.ncbi.nlm.nih.gov/2066374 2/

46. Ganatra B & Hirve S. Induced abortions among adolescent women in rural Maharashtra, India. Reproductive Health Matters. 2002 May; 10(19): 76–85. https://pubmed.ncbi.nlm.nih.gov/12369334/

47. Sowmini C V. Delay in termination of pregnancy among unmarried adolescents and young women attending a tertiary hospital abortion clinic in Trivandrum, Kerala, India. Reproductive Health Matters. 2013 May; 21(41): 243–250. https://pubmed.ncbi.nlm.nih.gov/23684207/

48. Mohamed S, Chipeta M.G., Kamninga T, Nthakomwa L, Chifungo C et al. Interventions to prevent unintended pregnancies among adolescents: a rapid overview of systematic reviews. Systematic Review. https://www.ncbi. nlm.nih.gov/pmc/articles/PMC10585784/

49. Chandrasekaran S, Chandrashekar VS, Dalvie S & Sinha A. The case for the use of telehealth for abortion in India. Sexual and Reproductive Health Matters. 2022 Jan 1; 29(2): 1920566. https://doi.org/10.1080/26410397.2021 .1920566

50. Sujay R. Premarital sexual behaviour among unmarried college students of Gujarat, India. Population Council. 2009. https://knowledgecommons.po pcouncil.org/departments_sbsr-rh/511

51. Singh I, Shukla A, Thulaseedharan JV & Singh G. Contraception for married adolescents (15–19 years) in India: Insights from the National family health survey-4 (NFHS-4). Reproductive Health. 2021 Dec 20; 18(1): 253. https://doi.org/10.1186/s12978-021-01310-9

52. Iyengar K, Klingberg Allvin M, Iyengar SD, Danielsson KG & Essén B. "Who Wants to Go Repeatedly to the Hospital?" Perceptions and Experiences of Simplified Medical Abortion in Rajasthan, India. Global Qualitative Nursing Research. 2016 Dec 19; 3:2333393616683073. https://www.ncbi.nlm.nih.gov/ pmc/articles/PMC5342849/

53. Data.gov.in. Open Government Data (OGD) Platform India. Data.gov.in.

2022. https://data.gov.in

54. Shukla A, Kumar A, Mozumdar A, Acharya R, Aruldas K & Saggurti N. Restrictions on contraceptive services for unmarried youth: a qualitative study of providers' beliefs and attitudes in India. 2022 Nov 23. https://www.tandfonline.com/doi/full/10.1080/26410397.2022.2141965

55. U.S. Department of Health & Human Services. Contraception and preventing pregnancy. U.S. Department of Health & Human Services Office of Population Affairs. https://opa.hhs.gov/reproductive-health/preventing-pregnancy-contraception

56. Vikaspedia. Contraception for adolescents. Vikaspedia. https://vikaspedia.in/health/women-health/adolescent-health-1/management-of-adolescent-health/contraception-for-adolescents

57. United Nations Children's Fund, United Nations Women and Plan International. A new era for girls; taking stock of 25 years of progress. United Nations Children's Fund. 2020 Mar. https://www.unicef.org/reports/new-era-for-girls-2020

58. Moseson H, Mahanaimy M, Dehlendorf C & Gerdts C. "...Society is, at the end of the day, still going to stigmatize you no matter which way": A qualitative study of the impact of stigma on social support during unintended pregnancy in early adulthood. PLoS ONE. 2019 May 23; 14(5). https://www.ncbi.nlm.nih.gov/pmc/articles/PMC6532899/

59. Rice WS, Turan B, Stringer KL, Helova A, White K, Cockrill K, et al. Norms and stigma regarding pregnancy decisions during an unintended pregnancy: Development and predictors of scales among young women in the U.S. South. PLoS ONE. 2017 Mar 22; 12(3). https://www.ncbi.nlm.nih.gov/pmc/articles/PMC5362217/

60. Smith W, Turan JM, White K, Stringer KL, Helova A, Simpson T, et al. Social norms and stigma regarding unintended pregnancy and pregnancy decisions: A qualitative study of young women in Alabama. Perspective on Sexual and Reproductive Health. 2016 Jun; 48(2): 73–81. https://www.ncbi.nlm.nih.gov/pmc/articles/PMC5022769/

61. Yakubu I & Salisu WJ. Determinants of adolescent pregnancy in sub-Saharan Africa: a systematic review. Reproductive Health. 2018 Jan 27; 15: 15.

https://www.ncbi.nlm.nih.gov/pmc/articles/PMC5787272/

62. International Institute for Population Sciences. National Family Health Survey (NFHS-3). Ministry of Health and Family Welfare Government of India. 2007 Sep. https://dhsprogram.com/pubs/pdf/frind3/frind3-vol1and vol2.pdf

63. Centers for Disease Control and Prevention. Condom Use: An Overview. Center for Diseases Control and Prevention. https://www.cdc.gov/condom-use/?CDC_AAref_Val=https://www.cdc.gov/condomeffectiveness/docs/condoms_and_stds.pdf

64. Vigneswaran E, Padmanabha R, Devanna N & JaffarSadiq M. Evaluation of Barriers on condom use - A cross sectional surveys. International Journal of Research in Pharmaceutical and Biomedical Sciences. 2011 Jan; 2(2): 510-515 https://www.researchgate.net/publication/264419428_Evaluation_of_Barriers_on_condom_use_-_A_cross_sectional_surveys

65. Jain M, Jain S, Patil S & Bang A. A study on knowledge attitude and practice of contraception in school going children in Wardha district in central India. International Journal of Reproductive, Contraception Obstetrics, and Gynaecology. 2014; 3(4): 903–908. https://www.ijrcog.org/index.php/ijrcog/article/view/1264

66. Deol T. Why is India's condom usage so low? First 'condomology' report notes social factors. The Print. 2021 May 29. https://theprint.in/feature/why-is-indias-condom-usage-so-low-first-condomology-report-notes-social-factors/667633/

67. Chandra J & Sen S. 'Only 1 in 10 men use condoms, female sterilisation most common contraceptive.' The Hindu. 2021 Nov 29. https://www.thehindu.com/news/national/only-1-in-10-men-use-condoms-female-sterilisation-most-common-contraceptive/article37758791.ece

68. Bhalla N. Condom use low amongst India's unmarried youth - study. Reuters. 2011 Dec 23. https://www.reuters.com/article/idUSDEE7BM04K/

69. World Health Organization. Global HIV programme: HIV testing services. World Health Organization. https://www.who.int/teams/global-hiv-hepatitis-and-stis-programmes/hiv/testing-diagnostics/hiv-testing-services

70. World Health Organization. Global HIV, Hepatitis and STIs Programmes. World Health Organization. https://www.who.int/teams/global-hiv-hepatitis-and-stis-programmes/populations

71. Program for Appropriate Technology in Health. HIV self-testing in India: Moving from evidence to action. Program for Appropriate Technology in Health. https://www.path.org/our-impact/resources/hiv-self-testing-/

72. World Health Organization. Global HIV programme: Pre-exposure prophylaxis (PrEP). World Health Organization. https://www.who.int/teams/global-hiv-hepatitis-and-stis-programmes/hiv/prevention/pre-exposure-prophylaxis

73. Chandra-Mouli V, McCarraher DR, Phillips SJ, Williamson NE & Hainsworth G. Contraception for adolescents in low- and middle-income countries: needs, barriers, and access. Reproductive Health. 2014 Jan 2;11: 1. https://www.ncbi.nlm.nih.gov/pmc/articles/PMC3882494/

74. Bill & Melinda Gates Foundation & United Nations Population Fund. Adding it up: The costs and benefits of investing in sexual and reproductive health 2014. United Nations Population Fund. 2014. https://www.unfpa.org/sites/default/files/pub-pdf/Adding%20It%20Up-Final-11.18.14.pdf

75. Vereinte Nationen, editor. Motherhood in childhood: Facing the challenge of adolescent pregnancy. United Nations Population Fund; State of World Population. 2013; 116. https://www.unfpa.org/sites/default/files/pub-pdf/EN-SWOP2013.pdf

76. World Health Organization. WHO Guidelines on Preventing Early Pregnancy and Poor Reproductive Health Outcomes Among Adolescents in Developing Countries. World Health Organization; Geneva. 2011. https://pubmed.ncbi.nlm.nih.gov/26180870/

77. Sample Registration System. SRS - Maternal Mortality Bulletin. Sample registration System. Government of India. 2022 Nov 28. https://censusindia.gov.in/census.website/data/SRSMMB

78. National AIDS Control Organization. National Behavioural Surveillance Survey (BSS). National AIDS Control Organization. 2006. https://naco.gov.in/sites/default/files/Youth_report_1.pdf

79. Population Foundation of India. Impact of COVID-19 on young people:

Rapid assessment in three states. 2020 May.https://www.populationfounda tion.in/wp-content/uploads/2020/08/Rapid-Assessment_Report_Youth_ Survey_Covid.pdf

80. Compromised Abortion Access due to COVID-19: A model to determine impact of COVID-19 on women's access to abortion – Ipas Development Foundation. 2020 May. Ipas Development Foundation. https://www.ipas developmentfoundation.org/archives/resources/compromised-abortion-a ccess-due-to-covid-19-a-model-to-determine-impact-of-covid-19-on-womens-access-to-abortion

81. Chandra-Mouli V, Parameshwar PS, Parry M, Lane C, Hainsworth G, Wong S, et al. A never-before opportunity to strengthen investment and action on adolescent contraception, and what we must do to make full use of it. Reproductive Health. 2017 Jul 20; 14(1): 85. https://doi.org/10.1186/ s12978-017-0347-9

82. Patel V, Ramasundarahettige C, Vijayakumar L, Thakur JS, Gajalakshmi V, Gururaj G, et al. Suicide mortality in India: a nationally representative survey. Lancet. 2012 Jun 23; 379(9834): 2343–2351. https://www.ncbi.nlm.n ih.gov/pmc/articles/PMC4247159/

83. Saxena S, Funk M & Chisholm D. WHO's Mental Health Action Plan 2013-2020: what can psychiatrists do to facilitate its implementation? World Psychiatry. 2014 Jun ;13(2):107–109. https://www.ncbi.nlm.nih.gov/pmc/ articles/PMC4102273/

84. Shidhaye R & Kermode M. Stigma and discrimination as a barrier to mental health service utilization in India. International Health. 2013 Mar; 5(1): 6–8. https://pubmed.ncbi.nlm.nih.gov/24029838/

85. Murthy RS. National Mental Health Survey of India 2015–2016. Indian Journal of Psychiatry. 2017; 59(1): 21–26. https://www.ncbi.nlm.nih.gov/ pmc/articles/PMC5419008/

86. Phulambrikar RM, Kharde AL, Mahavarakar VN, Phalke DB & Phalke VD. Effectiveness of interventional reproductive and sexual health educa-tion among school going adolescent girls in rural area. Indian Journal of Community Medicine Official Publication of Indian Association Preventive & Social Medicine. 2019; 44(4): 378–382. https://www.ncbi.nlm.nih.gov/pmc/

articles/PMC6881892/

87. Malhotra A, Amin A & Nanda P. Catalyzing gender norm change for adolescent sexual and reproductive health: Investing in interventions for structural change. Journal of Adolescent Health. 2019 Apr; 64(4 Suppl): 13–5. https://www.ncbi.nlm.nih.gov/pmc/articles/PMC6426763/

88. Patra S & Patro BK. COVID-19 and adolescent mental health in India. Lancet Psychiatry. 2020 Dec; 7(12): 1015. https://www.ncbi.nlm.nih.gov/pmc/articles/PMC8869558/

89. Javed B, Sarwer A, Soto EB & Mashwani Z ur-Rehman. The coronavirus (COVID-19) pandemic's impact on mental health. International Journal of Health Planning and Management. 2020 Sep; 35(5): 993. https://www.ncbi.nlm.nih.gov/pmc/articles/PMC7361582/

90. Ferguson L, Fried S, Matsaseng T, Ravindran S & Gruskin S. Human rights and legal dimensions of self care interventions for sexual and reproductive health. The British Medical Journal. 2019 May 13; 365:l1941. https://www.ncbi.nlm.nih.gov/pmc/articles/PMC6511940/

91. United Nations Population Fund India. Investing in young people. United Nations Population Fund India. https://india.unfpa.org/sites/default/files/pub-pdf/UNFPAProfile2013_Final%20%281%29.pdf

92. Byers E.S., Sullivan L O, Mitra K & Sears H.A. Parent-adolescent sexual communication in India: Responses of middle class parents. Journal of Family Issues. 2020 Jun; 42(4). https://www.researchgate.net/publication/342132704_Parent-Adolescent_Sexual_Communication_in_India_Responses_of_Middle_Class_Parents

93. Raman S. Abortion is legal in india but rules, stigma make it hard to access. BehanBox https://behanbox.com/2022/05/09/abortion-is-legal-in-india-but-rules-stigma-make-it-hard-to-access/

94. Population Foundation of India. The sexual & reproductive health status of young people in India. Population Foundation of India. https://india.unfpa.org/sites/default/files/pub-pdf/brief2_-_the_srh_status_of_young_people.pdf

95. Das JK, Salam RA, Lassi ZS, Khan MN, Mahmood W, Patel V, et al. Interventions for Adolescent Mental Health: An Overview of Systematic

Reviews. Journal of Adolescent Health. 2016 Oct; 59(4 Suppl): 49–60. https://www.ncbi.nlm.nih.gov/pmc/articles/PMC5026677/

96. Stalin P. Emotional intelligence in health care. Journal of Current Research Scientific Medicine. 2024 Jun; 10(1):1-2. https://journals.lww.com/jcsm/fulltext/2024/10010/emotional_intelligence_in_health_care.1.aspx

Breaking Boundaries: Rachna's Journey Through Tradition, Health, and Self-Empowerment

This story is about Rachna Kumari, a 23-year-old strong and independent college graduate with a determined mind. She came from a small town called Pathanamthitta in Kerala, India where she lived with her family. Rachna identifies herself as bisexual and is currently single. She is well aware of her sexual and reproductive health and rights. She is proactive and conscious about her health. She is still exploring life, getting to know herself, and discovering her sexuality while challenging the norms of society and of her traditional Indian family. In addition to these challenges, she is struggling with anemia. She was diagnosed with PCOS (polycystic ovary syndrome) in her early twenties.

Even though she understands sexual and reproductive health matters, Rachna never sought professional services, especially while she was involved with a female partner. She expressed concerns about her lack of information on HIV and self-sampling for STIs. She believes that it is possible to access self-care products at various pharmacies. Most of Rachna's information on sexual health is derived from social magazines like *Vanita* and *Manorama*, as well as through blogs where people share their personal experiences about sexual health and access to self-care products. Rachna tracks her monthly periods regularly. She finds this a convenient way to manage her health. She believes that digital tools and other informal sources have provided her with insights and guidance. She feels she can better relate to them than formal healthcare channels. She trusts in peer-reviewed articles and makes health decisions only after consulting with friends with expertise in related fields, as she values their input over conventional medical advice.

Rachna is reluctant to seek formal healthcare, which is a hesitation she expressed when discussing her discomfort with visiting healthcare facilities. She said, *"When I accompany my friends to buy hormonal pills, the first question the store clerk asks is 'Is it for pregnancy?'"* She also recalled her visit to a doctor when she was 19 or 20 years old. This doctor told her mother, *"Marriage is a long-term solution for hormonal imbalance and pregnancy."* The treatment approach followed by doctors for PCOS treatment did not suit her. She felt lost and overwhelmed during the treatment. Doctors suggested marriage as her better treatment plan, which she found unacceptable. This focus on marriage created distress and stigma. Rachna was hesitant to visit healthcare facilities because she faced stigma at these facilities. Rachna prefers to share her experiences with friends rather than with her family members about such sensitive issues. She shared her thoughts on intimacy, saying, *"Sex is a very intimate thing. If you contract infection, it might become chronic. So, I believe one needs to take proper precautions."*

Rachna shared her thoughts about how challenging it is to be born into a traditional Indian family. In many traditional Indian families, elders within the family decide when their children should have kids—a decision that Rachna feels is deeply personal and should be made by the individual, especially by the woman. She shared an experience where her mother questioned a friend about not using protection, reflecting the traditional belief that marriage plans often include the expectation of immediate pregnancy. Rachna noted, *"According to my mother, people plan their marriages with the expectation of getting pregnant soon, and using protection on the first night of marriage is unacceptable."* She expressed that this attitude creates a judgmental pressure on women who may not wish to conceive immediately after marriage.

Earlier, Rachna lived in a hostel, where her life was very different. But the COVID-19 pandemic changed everything. It disrupted her sense of stability and independence, forcing her to return to her hometown. There, her freedom was restricted. During her college years, she enjoyed a life free from the constraints of societal norms. But the pandemic brought back all the challenges she thought she had left behind. Due to financial problems, she had to leave the hostel, and with that, her independence was once again curtailed by societal restrictions. She discussed the constraints she faced as a woman living within society, describing how difficult it can be to navigate everyday life. She said that women often face resistance in many aspects of their lives, saying, *"We have a curfew for going out at odd hours...We have to be back home before evening. It's hard to get permission to travel. We always face resistance."* This reflected the struggles that she faced. She feels that societal norms and expectations limit a woman's ability to lead a life on her terms.

Rachna also shared her frustration about the lack of autonomy in her own life. Despite wanting to make decisions for herself, especially concerning her reproductive health, she found that her mother usually made these decisions. She felt compelled to follow her mother's directions, even when they conflicted with her desires or needs. This took a toll on her mental health. Rachna felt stressed. The grief and emotional challenges she experienced were traumatic. She sought external support to navigate the obstacles. She later joined a mental health peer group—a safe space—where she could openly share her problems without any judgment and could piece together the fragments of her disrupted life.

Amidst all the stigmas and challenges Rachna faced, she realized, *"One needs to take care of oneself before one can take care of others. If you don't take care of yourself first, you see it as a problem, and you start blaming others."* This reshaped her perspective on life. She became conscious, mindful, and understanding of herself and others. Rachna believes that self-awareness and self-care are the foundation for healthy relationships. She recognizes that physical affection and emotional support are not just personal needs, they also bind people together. This fosters a change in one's outlook on society. Rachna believes raising awareness is a crucial first step for bringing comfort and security to the family and community. She thinks it is important to pay attention to one's health and self-care. Only then can we take care of others.

Self-Care Experiences of High School Students and College Graduates in the USA

Saroj Pachauri, Public Health Specialist, Trustee, Center for Human Progress, New Delhi, India, and Director, POP (Protect Our Planet) Movement, New York, USA

Ash Pachauri, Director, Center for Human Progress, New Delhi, India, and Senior Mentor, POP (Protect Our Planet) Movement, New York, USA

Komal Mittal, Research Associate, Center for Human Progress, New Delhi, India and Youth Mentor, POP (Protect Our Planet) Movement, New York, USA

Drishya Pathak, Research Associate, Center for Human Progress, New Delhi, India and Youth Mentor, POP (Protect Our Planet) Movement, New York, USA

Abstract

In the USA, sexual and reproductive health (SRH) enables informed decisions on childbearing, abortion, sexually transmitted infections (STIs), and sexual behaviors. Self-care interventions improve SRH by enhancing accessibility and autonomy while reducing public health service dependence. The 2019 WHO guideline emphasizes self-care practices like self-medication and self-testing. High rates of unsafe abortion and rising AIDS-related deaths highlight the need for comprehensive SRH interventions. In this chapter, the authors highlight that there is a significant research gap on SRH self-care practices among young people in the USA. Addressing this gap is crucial for developing effective interventions and improving healthcare quality.

Background

Sexual and reproductive health (SRH) enables individuals to make choices and decisions about childbearing, abortion, sexual practices, sexually transmitted infections (STIs), including HIV, and sexual behaviors (1).

Self-care can improve accessibility of sexual and reproductive health information and services. It can reduce over-dependence on public health services especially for people who do not have access to these services. It can facilitate healthcare accessibility and increase people's understanding of their health and wellbeing (2).

Self-care interventions have emerged as an important tool for empowering people to take charge of their own health and wellbeing. By enabling individuals to make informed decisions about their sexual and reproductive health, self-care interventions improve autonomy, reduce barriers to access, and improve health outcomes.

The publication of the first comprehensive guideline on self-care interventions for health and wellbeing by the World Health Organization (WHO) in 2019 marked a significant milestone in the field of sexual and reproductive health and rights (SRHR) (3). This guideline prioritizes self-care practices that promote overall health and wellbeing, including, but not limited to, self-medication, self-injection, self-testing, self-sampling, self-monitoring, and educational initiatives. For example, self-medication enables people to manage minor health problems and alleviates symptoms without their having to seek formal health services. Self-care not only provides convenience and cost-saving benefits but also fosters a sense of self-efficacy and responsibility for one's own health, including sexual and reproductive health. It, thereby, paves the way for improved health outcomes. It also reduces barriers to access and fosters autonomy.

According to the United Nations International Children's Emergency Fund

(UNICEF) report on monitoring the evaluation of children and women, a staggering number of young girls, approximately 3.9 million aged 15 to 19 years, undergo unsafe abortions annually. It is alarming to note that one in every four girls gives birth during her adolescent years or before she turns 18 (4). Males are vulnerable to infectious diseases, especially sexually transmitted infections (STIs). Unintended pregnancy rates are related to the socioeconomic status of young people (5). In the United States, approximately 13 percent of the young population is between 18 to 24 years of age and 21.64 million young people are between the ages of 15 to 19 years as per the 2022 available data (6). However, because the demography of youth is constantly changing, it is important to pay attention to their needs on an ongoing basis.

Sexual and reproductive health (SRH) has traditionally focused on pregnancy, abortion, and STIs. Recent studies indicate that self-care should form an integral component of SRH. This shift in focus recognizes the importance of empowering individuals to take charge of their own health and wellbeing. The 2018 Inter-Agency Working Group highlighted the concerning trend in AIDS-related mortality rates. Between the years 2000 and 2014, deaths associated with AIDS witnessed a significant increase from 21,000 to 60,000 (1). Projections indicate that this situation is likely to worsen if adequate measures are not taken. Considering these alarming statistics, it is evident that there is an urgent need for comprehensive and targeted interventions to address multiple sexual and reproductive health challenges. Interventions should not only focus on preventative measures but should also emphasize the promotion of safe and accessible options for individuals seeking SRH services. Efforts should be made to increase awareness and enhance access to self-care products and services like contraceptives and STI treatment to reduce unwanted pregnancy and prevent morbidity particularly among adolescents and young adults (4).

High numbers of unsafe abortions, adolescent pregnancies, and AIDS-related deaths highlight the urgent need for providing comprehensive interventions that prioritize education, access to contraception, and to health services.

Through concerted efforts, we can strive towards a future where individuals are empowered with the knowledge and means to make informed decisions about their sexual and reproductive health. This will ultimately lead to healthier and more empowered communities. Health systems must prioritize the provision of accurate information, counseling services, medical resources, and support networks to ensure that young people, both male and female, receive timely and appropriate care. By empowering individuals with knowledge and resources, self-care for SRH is an alternative means for reducing the prevalence of unsafe abortion, early pregnancy, and STIs.

Methodology

A qualitative research study was undertaken in five states— Florida, Texas, New York, New Jersey, California, and Iowa in the USA. Qualitative research methods allow greater spontaneity and interaction with the research participants. They provide an opportunity for the participants to respond elaborately and in greater detail which provides a more nuanced understanding of the issues.

Data was collected online and offline by conducting in-depth interviews (IDIs), focus group discussions (FGDs), and workshops with high school students and college graduates (married and unmarried). The questionnaires were aligned with WHO's Self-care Values and Preferences Survey, which was administered globally (4). However, our study included additional components on gender norms, mental health, and COVID-19.

The interviews were conducted using interview guides. The interviews were approximately 90-120 minutes in length and were audio recorded using an external device. Audio recordings were transcribed and checked for accuracy. Eight IDIs and two FGDs were conducted with college graduates (19-28 years of age). One in-depth interview was conducted with a gay college graduate, three with bisexual female college graduates, one with a non-binary, one with a pansexual, and one with a college graduate who did not know his/her sexuality.

Ethical approval for undertaking the study was granted by the Institutional Review Board of Sigma (Sigma-IRB), Sigma Research and Consulting, New Delhi, India. Before conducting the research interviews, the interviewer described the objectives and importance of the study to all research participants. Participants were given consent forms that described the study risks and potential harm. They were assured that the study posed minimal or no quantifiable harm to their physical or mental wellbeing. They were also told they could skip any questions that they did not wish to answer and that they could withdraw consent at any point during the interview, following which the data would be destroyed. Written and verbal consent was obtained from all participants. Confidentiality of the study participants was assured.

Transcripts were thoroughly read and some unique similarities and differences were identified in the data collected. Based on this, a number of themes were used as probes for analysis. The themes included service provision, knowledge, attitudes, and behavior, scope, condom use, sexually transmitted infections (STIs) including HIV/AIDS, pregnancy, and empowerment through social support networks. Quotes were generously used to amplify the voices of the research participants and to highlight the research results.

Literature review

A literature search was carried out across multiple databases, including PubMed, British Medical Journal (BMJ), the World Health Organization (WHO), PubMed Central (PMC), Sage Journals, Guttmacher Institute, Science Direct, Springer, Taylor & Francis, Wiley Online Library, Centers for Disease Control (CDC), Elsevier, Pew Research Center, National Institute of Health, and others. A variety of search terms and keywords were used for the research. These included young, youth, adolescent, young adult, self-care, sexual and reproductive health, abortion, unintended pregnancy, self-sampling, self-management, mental health problems, stress, depression, suicide, alcohol, tobacco use, substance use, and violence.

Literature on self-care is notably sparse, particularly for young people in the USA. The authors encountered a significant dearth of research focused on self-care practices pertaining to sexual and reproductive health of young people. Despite the pressing need for understanding and promoting self-care for sexual and reproductive health, available research addressing this issue is very limited. This suggests that there is an urgent need to undertake research on self-care practices especially on those concerning sexual and reproductive health and rights of young people in the USA. This research is needed for designing effective interventions for self-care and also for improving the overall quality of healthcare.

Risky sexual behaviors among young people in the USA

Several statistical models suggest that adolescents and young people have increased levels of vulnerability to different health conditions, including sexual and reproductive health. Early pregnancy occurred in 870,000 adolescents 15 to 19 years of age. There were three million cases of sexually transmitted diseases (STDs) among 10 to 19-year-olds. Early pregnancy, STIs, and HIV infections before age 25 were some of the leading conditions related to risky sexual behaviors (7). When compared with older adults, sexually active adolescents aged 15-19 years were at a higher risk of acquiring sexually transmitted infections due to behavioral, biological, and cultural reasons (8). Socioeconomic status, joblessness, family instability, single-parent households, siblings' sexual activity, and other characteristics (race, gender, age, and puberty) were associated with risky sexual behavior (9). In a survey conducted in 2021 among U.S. high school students, it was found that 30 percent of the students had experienced sexual intercourse at least once, and 48 percent had not used a condom during their most recent sexual encounter. Eight percent reported being coerced into sexual intercourse against their will. Only nine percent of the students had undergone HIV testing (10).

The National Survey of Family Growth (NSFG) in never-married adolescents documented that a sizable proportion of females were engaged in penile-vaginal intercourse. However, there was a decline in this behavior among males (11). According to a study by Lindberg, trends in sexual behavior among young people showed that in 2015-2019, more than half of adolescents (54% females, 52% males) had had some sexual experience. For both genders, penile-vaginal intercourse (41% females, 39% males) or oral sex with a partner of a different sex (44% females, 43% males) was more common than anal sex with a partner of a different sex (9% females, 8% males) or sexual experience with a same-sex partner (15% females, 3% males) (11). Previous research data published by the Centers for Disease Control (CDC) in 2020 showed similar findings. Young people aged 13-24 years accounted for 20 percent of all new HIV cases in the US. Of the 20 million new STDs reported in 2020, more than half were reported among young people. However, from 2011 to 2021, there was a decrease in risky sexual behavior among high school students, which resulted in lowering their risk for HIV, STDs, and unintended pregnancy (12).

While the rates of drug use fluctuate annually, recent data underscores the continuing challenge of substance abuse among young adults. In 2018, an estimated 34.1 million individuals aged 18 to 25 were living in the United States. As per the 2018 National Survey on Drug Use and Health, over one-third of these young adults reported binge drinking (consuming five or more alcoholic beverages consecutively) within the past month, with approximately two in five reporting the use of illicit drugs within the preceding year (13).

Notably, one in ten young adults met the criteria for an alcohol use disorder, while one in seven grappled with a substance use disorder (14). One in thirteen exhibited symptoms of an illicit drug use disorder, with one in seventeen experiencing challenges related to marijuana use and one in hundred facing an opioid use disorder. Drug use has been linked to adverse outcomes, including increased risk of persistent drug misuse, academic underachievement, impaired decision-making, heightened vulnerability to accidents, violence, unprotected sexual activity, and suicidal ideation among youth (15).

Research exploring the nexus between substance use and sexual behavior among adolescents revealed a correlation between the two phenomena. Factors such as ever engaging in sexual activity, having multiple sexual partners, inconsistent condom usage, and early pregnancy (before the age of 15) were associated with substance use among adolescents. Studies have also indicated a positive relationship between the frequency of substance use and the likelihood of engaging in risky sexual behaviors as well as having a number of sexual partners. Alcohol use has been linked to increased sexual risk-taking among adolescents, with heightened risk among those who use drugs and other illicit substances. Conversely, teens abstaining from substance use are least likely to engage in risky sex behaviors (16). For instance, alcohol consumption by adolescents was associated with a 3.37-fold increase in the likelihood of having more than three sexual partners, with male adolescents exhibiting a 2.9-fold increase in the likelihood compared to their female counterparts (16).

Data from the 2017 Youth Risk Behavior Surveillance System (YRBSS) revealed that 40 percent of high school students had experienced intercourse, with 29 percent currently engaging in sexual activity. Among sexually active students, 19 percent reported alcohol or drug use preceding their last sexual encounter (17).

Socioeconomic and cultural barriers

Improving sexual and reproductive health (SRH) is crucial for the overall wellbeing of young adults. Numerous cultural and socioeconomic barriers impede accessibility to services and products. These include factors such as confidentiality, stigma, discrimination, fear, cost, accessibility, prejudice, stereotype, legal restrictions, jurisdiction, knowledge gaps, and family background. Understanding these challenges is vital for advancing the sexual and reproductive health and rights of young people. Several socioeconomic and cultural factors affect contraceptive use and, therefore, impact SRH of youth. The US has significant ethnic, cultural, and religious diversity, due to which there are conflicting views on sexuality, ultimately reflecting reproductive life (18).

In a survey conducted by Guttmacher in 2011, it was found that unintended pregnancy rates were significantly higher in the US as compared to other developed countries. Approximately five percent of reproductive-age (15-44 years) women had an unintended pregnancy. This rate was higher among women aged 18-24 years and for those from the lowest socioeconomic strata. This proportion decreased with age. The highest unintended pregnancy rate of 81 per 1,000 women was observed in the 20-24 years age group (19). These findings indicate that socioeconomic status has a major role to play in adopting healthy sexual and reproductive behaviors.

The US is well known for having a diverse population that includes African American, Asian, Hispanic, and others. This diversity is continuously increasing (20). These diverse population groups belong to different religions and ethnicities, which have different impacts on their sexual and reproductive decisions. A study conducted by Miller in 2014 to understand sexual and reproductive behavior of adolescents with a mean age of 15 years, where 90 percent of participants were African Americans, showed that 30 percent had not used a condom at last intercourse. Among those who reported previous sexual activity, 30 percent reported that they had never talked with a parent or guardian about STIs and pregnancy prevention (21).

Addressing cultural and socioeconomic barriers faced by young people in accessing SRH services and products is crucial for the advancement of sexual and reproductive health and rights. Measures such as ensuring confidentiality, challenging stigma and discrimination, providing affordable and accessible services, addressing knowledge gaps, and promoting an open dialogue within families could serve as important tools for empowering young people to take control of their SRH and, thereby, contribute to their overall wellbeing. It is the responsibility of society, healthcare providers, policy-makers, and educational institutions to work collectively to remove these barriers and to create an environment for promoting young people's SRH.

Sexual consent and legal age of marriage

In the United States, the issues of marriage and sexual consent are governed by state law, which establishes the acceptable parameters for marriage within each state. While child marriage is strictly prohibited in the United States, individuals who are 18 years and older can legally enter into marriage depending on the marriage age laws of their specific states. This can be done with or without the consent of their parents, as determined by state regulations. It is important to note that all states in the U.S. have a legal age for marriage and sex, commonly referred to as the "age of consent," which signifies the age at which individuals can legally agree to become spouses without requiring parental permission. This age requirement varies from state to state. In most states, the minimum age for marriage is 18 years. However, there are exceptions, such as Mississippi and Puerto Rico, where the minimum age is 21. In Nebraska, the minimum age is 19 years (22). Similarly, the age of sexual consent also varies from state to state albeit within a specific range. This age typically ranges from 16 to 18 years, depending on the legal age of consent (23).

It is important to examine the specific laws and regulations of each state to fully understand marriage age requirements and sexual consent laws in particular jurisdictions. By doing so, individuals can ensure that they are acting within the legal boundaries established by their respective states.

Knowledge and practice of self-care for SRH among young people

Non-use of contraception or use of less effective methods or inconsistent use of contraceptives are risky behaviors that can result in unintended pregnancies. These behaviors are more likely to occur in teenagers than in older women. And, they vary among populations of different ethnicities and races. Factors that influence the use of contraceptives are misinformation and misperceptions regarding the effects, side-effects, and effectiveness of the methods. There are other indicators that affect access to knowledge of self-care interventions. The National Survey on Reproductive and Contraceptive Knowledge found racial and ethnic differences in attitudes about contraception, pregnancy, and fertility (24). A study was undertaken by Amaranta et al in 2014 to examine the knowledge and attitudes to contraceptives among populations from different demographic groups belonging to different ethnicity, race, and age. It showed that there were substantial deficits in the awareness of contraceptive methods and method-specific knowledge. Differences in knowledge and practice were found to vary among different demographic groups. Knowledge about condoms was almost universal (24). However, there was a lower awareness and incomplete knowledge among teenagers as compared to adults on self-managed contraceptives (birth control pills, female barrier methods, natural family planning methods, emergency contraception), and other contraceptive methods (24).

A report published by Guttmacher in 2018 analyzed data from the Centers for Disease Control for 2013, 2015, and 2017 on high school students. The report focused on sexual activity, contraceptive use, STIs, HIV, and adolescent pregnancy. There was a visible decline in pregnancy rates among 15-19-year-old adolescents and those above this age. Between 2000 and 2014, there was a visible decline in abortions at this age group (25). It was also found that from 2012 to 2016 there was a significant increase in the rates of STIs including chlamydia, gonorrhea, and syphilis among 15-24-year-old males. This report indicated that most sexually active high school students used contraceptives. According to the 2017 data, 16 percent of sexually active females and 10 percent of males reported that they or their partner had not used any method to prevent pregnancy. These sexually active females and males were mostly from the ninth, 11th, and 12th-grades (25).

Self-managed pregnancies, abortions, contraceptive use, and sexually transmitted infections

Pregnancy and contraceptive use

Adolescents in the United States face a high risk of unintended pregnancy and abortion. Annually, approximately 750,000 adolescents in the United States become pregnant with over 80 percent of these pregnancies being unintended. Almost a third of teens choose to terminate their pregnancies with either medication or an in-office procedure. The US Food and Drug Administration (FDA) approved mifepristone in 2000. Most adolescents use home pregnancy test kits when they suspect pregnancy. However, they are at a higher risk of getting false negatives due to developmental issues and greater variation in their menstrual cycles. Home pregnancy testing kits for adolescents should be highly sensitive and accurate (26). A study conducted by Shew et al. in 2000 estimated the prevalence of home pregnancy testing among 600 female adolescents (13 and 19 years of age) in 11 urban clinics. The study showed that there was a 34 percent prevalence of home pregnancy test use. Of those tested, 77 percent of adolescents mentioned that they had at least one false negative pregnancy test result. Forty eight percent of them had not taken any further action for pregnancy confirmation. These users were younger at sexual debut, less likely to use effective birth control, and more likely to have ever been pregnant (27). This placed them at the risk of unintended pregnancies. Efforts to address these issues, a US public health priority, are focused on reducing adolescent sexual activity and increasing contraceptive use (28). Notably, birth rates among youth aged 15–19 years have decreased to record lows in the US, which is partly attributed to the increased use of various contraceptive methods, including intrauterine devices (IUDs) and implants, which are also known as long-acting reversible contraceptives (29).

Studies on the use of medical abortion among adolescents in the US show satisfactory outcomes (30). A study by the Pew Research Center in 2023 showed that younger adults, particularly those under 30 years of age, expressed greater support for legalizing medical abortion compared to older people (25).

In 2020, medical abortions accounted for 53 percent of all facility-based abortions in the United States, according to data from both the Centers for Disease Control and Prevention and the Guttmacher Institute (31). Disparities persisted across racial/ethnic, geographic, and socioeconomic lines, as evidenced by higher birth rates among non-Hispanic black and Hispanic adolescents compared to non-Hispanic white adolescents (32).

Although they are less effective for pregnancy prevention, condoms remain vital for preventing STDs/HIV (33). Consistent condom use among African American adolescents remains a challenge. They show lower rates of recent condom use compared to their white or Hispanic counterparts (34).

Analysis of data from the Youth Risk Behavior Survey for the years 2013, 2015, and 2017 highlights improvements in contraceptive use among sexually active high school students (25). However, a notable percentage reported non-use of contraceptives during their last intercourse, particularly those from certain racial and ethnic backgrounds and younger students. Over this five-year period, there was a gradual decline in condom use among high school students (from 59% in 2013 to 54% in 2017). When examined by gender, race, and ethnicity, a significant decrease was observed in condom use among black males and white females (25). A number of studies have examined the role of parent-adolescent communication about sexual risk and its association with the use of condoms. Better parental communication on sexual risk and condom use is associated with increased use of condoms in adolescents (35).

Abortion

The Internet has become a vital resource for many individuals in the US for seeking information about self-abortion. Between 2011 and 2015, the number of Google searches in the US related to self-abortion increased from 119,000 to 700,000 (36). However, it was unclear if these Google searches were for ending their own pregnancies (36). While some young people seek self-managed abortion because they have limited access to healthcare facilities, others have a preference for self-care for its convenience, accessibility, and privacy (37).

Medical abortion with mifepristone and misoprostol constitutes more than half of all abortions in the US— at least 63 percent of abortions— and is increasingly under scrutiny (38)(39). It is the subject of a Supreme Court case that makes it illegal and much harder to access (40). The Supreme Court overturned the constitutionally protected right to access abortion, leaving the question of whether and how to regulate abortion (41). As of January 17, 2023, legal developments in abortion laws have led to abortion bans in thirteen states in the US (41). This affects approximately 22 million women and girls of reproductive age in the US. Despite these restrictions, medical abortion remains a safe and effective way to terminate pregnancy, particularly among young people. It is the most common method of abortion in high-income countries (42). Studies indicate that there is a high level of interest in self-abortion in the United States, particularly among young people (43).

A study by the Guttmacher Institute reveals a predominantly female demographic for seeking abortion with a significant number being minors— 80 percent were younger than 25 years— highlighting the importance of online resources for information and support. Since 2020, the emergence of a new type of abortion provider— online-only clinics— has further expanded medical abortion services. There has been a steady increase in their numbers(44). Online clinics have come to play an important role in abortion access, accounting for more than eight percent of all abortions provided nationwide (45).

According to the Pew Research Center, at least four in ten young people in the

US experienced mental health problems during the first wave of the COVID-19 pandemic (46). A concerning trend emerged, revealing the mental health struggles of young girls and women. Research showed that thousands of them stocked up on abortion pills as a precautionary measure, thinking that there might be access restrictions during the pandemic period (47). This behavior reflects anxieties among young people about the accessibility of healthcare products and reproductive health services. The surge in demand for abortion pills among young girls and women during the pandemic serves as a reminder of the intricate interplay between mental health and sexual health needs resulting from societal pressure and underscores the need for developing support systems.

When it comes to the use of abortion pills, knowledge regarding the safety, effectiveness, expected outcomes, and complications is of utmost priority to ensure that pregnant teenagers and youth receive accurate counseling. Not only should youth be made aware of abortion pills, but healthcare providers should also be better educated on medical abortion. In a study conducted by Mandy et al. in 2011 in which 797 adolescents were surveyed, 96 percent of providers offered pregnancy tests, and 78 percent referred the adolescents for abortion services. Half of the providers were familiar with medical abortion. More than a quarter reported being "not too familiar" and eight percent were "not at all familiar" with the mifepristone regimen. More than half of the providers who responded had incorrect knowledge about the expected outcomes, effects, and complications. The study identified serious gaps in the knowledge of medical abortion among healthcare providers (48).

Self-sampling and self-testing

Approximately 1.2 million people in the United States are living with HIV. Around 158,500 people are unaware of their status. Nearly 40 percent of new HIV infections are transmitted by people who are not aware that they are infected. Early detection through testing is crucial for maintaining a healthy life and preventing HIV transmission (49).

Research indicates that many people find self-testing acceptable and sometimes preferable to in-person testing. Studies show that people can accurately administer rapid self-tests and interpret results correctly. Self-testing is particularly effective in vulnerable populations such as gay and bisexual men and people who seldom access HIV testing services. It is also cost-effective and helps to overcome barriers that prevent in-person HIV testing. By increasing privacy, confidentiality, and anonymity, self-testing addresses the problem of stigma and discrimination which prevents people from seeking in-person HIV testing (50)(51)(52)(53). CDC recommends that everyone between the ages of 13 and 64 years should get tested for HIV at least once as a part of routine health care (49).

Research Findings

The findings include a discussion of the life history of college graduates, their sexual behavior, their sexual activity with intimate partners, casual sex partners, self-care interventions adopted for SRHR, information sources of SRHR, risks and barriers faced by youth, motivations for self-care, and young people's health-related experiences during the pandemic.

Sexual behavior of youth

Most adolescents aged 19 and above who took part in the study were sexually active. Many of them, who provided detailed insights into their sex lives, reported being involved in more than three to four sexual relationships in the past. They emphasized prioritizing both their own and their partners' sexual and reproductive health and practicing self-care. For many participants, the use of contraceptives served as a means of preventing unwanted pregnancy. On average, the study participants admitted to having knowledge of atleast three to four contraceptive methods to avoid unwanted pregnancy and most of them had used at least two to three contraceptive self-care interventions. However, some of them shared their past experiences and their risky sexual behaviors as teenagers. When reflecting on their sexual and reproductive health experiences during the COVID pandemic period, participants indicated that their choices had remained unaffected.

"Yes, I am aware of birth control and abortion pills. I have had two early abortions too. Both pregnancies happened accidentally. I had sex with strangers while heavily drunk."

A 24-year-old sexually active female bisexual

Self-care interventions for sexual and reproductive health and rights

Perceptions of self-care

Participants underscored the importance of self-care for physical, mental, and spiritual health. They had a multifaceted understanding of health and wellbeing. They highlighted that proper nutrition, exercise, and engaging in activities like nature walks and breathing exercises are essential for good health. This holistic perspective acknowledges the interconnectedness of the mind, body, and spirit in achieving overall wellbeing. They described engaging in activities that brought them peace of mind and positively impacted their sexual and mental health. They felt that spending time with loved ones and pursuing one's interests contribute to mental wellbeing. By recognizing the interconnectedness of physical, mental, and spiritual wellbeing and advocating for personalized self-care practices, individuals can foster holistic wellbeing and address their unique needs.

"It's not just about getting nutrition. Self-care is subtle. It means feeling complete. It is need-based. I may have all the resources, nutrition, good health, and proper healthcare, but I may not be happy. Other factors play a role in my wellbeing. It's about understanding yourself and having a connection with yourself."

A 29-year-old gay post-graduate student

"Self-care is doing things that make you feel good and positively affect your sexual and mental health. I prioritize things that give me peace of mind like painting

and cooking with my mom and also taking care of myself…working out in my room…doing my skincare…all of my ways of taking care."

A 24-year-old sexually active female college graduate

Several participants noted that self-care, originally a natural aspect of life, has now become commercialized by industries aiming to profit from it. They mentioned how individual self-care in the US was increasingly being influenced by industries which poses challenges for people to afford self-care and manage it effectively.

"The self-care industry is very predatory where they market it to people that need it and then do branding and add subscription services like incense sticks. This is causing more financial distress. People are digging themselves deeper because of not having enough time or money to do things that would make them happy naturally."

A 25-year-old sexually active heterosexual male college graduate

"Self-care is important. Marketing is really funky, constantly buying something, surface level things. Sometimes it's systemic and out of control and sometimes it is in our control. The world is such shit. The first-year therapist was shitty but was fun to talk to. But now I have a really good therapist and she's been really good and things are really slowly down. I am stepping back to look at my relationships and to check-on what I am doing."

A 23-year-old sexually active pansexual female

Self-care interventions

The study revealed that college graduates had a varied range of perspectives on the type of SRH interventions they used. With respect to self-care interventions, college graduates preferred to use contraceptives such as condoms, birth control pills, hormonal implants, plan B (over-the-counter emergency contraception), IUDs, self-testing interventions for pregnancies and STIs, self-management interventions for menstrual hygiene, including the use of lubricants and abortion pills. College graduates exhibited a range of attitudes towards these practices, which were influenced by various factors that affected their knowledge and utilization of these products.

"IUD, it really works for me, I don't get a period at all, no cramps— grateful to not think about it a lot."

A 26-year-old sexually active female college graduate

Contraceptives

The study showed that the majority of college graduates and/or their partners used at least one contraceptive method. The most commonly used contraceptive method among the college graduates was the condom, which was mentioned by sexually active heterosexual males and heterosexual females. They said that condoms prevent both pregnancy and STIs. They also mentioned practising good hygiene, using contraceptives, and consulting healthcare professionals.

"One should use condoms when having sexual intercourse and maintain good hygiene. One should consult a doctor and take all precautions."

A 29-year-old gay post-graduate student

The second most commonly used contraceptive method among college graduates was birth control pills. This was mentioned by sexually active bisexual females, heterosexual females, bisexual non-binaries, and also by the partners of heterosexual males. Some college graduates discussed the side-effects of birth control pills. For example, a 24-year-old sexually active female college graduate mentioned, *"Used it in the past and didn't like the fact it was causing headaches and mood swings. I will never use it. It caused a lot of complications like blood clots."* Participants also shared their experiences of transitioning from birth control pills to other contraceptive methods.

"There is no stigma or judgment. I don't feel judged. Used until the first year of

141

college."

A 26-year-old sexually active female bisexual

"Yeah, in the past year, I had a weird reaction to birth control, and I stopped taking it, and now it's all weird. I went to a Catholic school so 'no contraception allowed' was the message. I went for a day-long seminar where they talked about the sins of contraception."

A 23-year-old sexually active female, pansexual college graduate

While sharing their attitudes towards contraceptives, some of the participants mentioned that they had used condoms and birth control pills. Additionally, the fact that some were covered by their insurance motivated them to use contraceptives.

"Used IUD. Contraception is paid by insurance."

A 26-year-old sexually active female bisexual

Self-testing interventions

The study revealed that college graduates used self-testing and self-sampling interventions like pregnancy test kits, HPV testing kits, STI testing kits and HIV testing kits. Only three college graduates said that they were aware of HIV self-testing kits or STIs self-sampling kits that can be accessed online. They highlighted the challenges associated with obtaining accurate samples and cautioned against relying on antigen tests for HIV diagnosis. They recommended the use of the ELISA method for accurate results. These individuals were mostly masters of public health (MPH) students.

"Self- sampling is as accurate as the real test. It is difficult to take samples. Not everybody is trained to do so. So, if you have a false negative result then it is difficult. Antigen tests for something like HIV can give a false sense of safety, so I would like to advise you to get the ELISA test done."

A 29-year-old bisexual female MBBS student

College graduates expressed feeling empowered as they had access to pregnancy test kits, *"It makes you feel good to know things about yourself and your pregnancy."*

Self-management interventions

College graduates used self-management interventions such as menstrual products, lubricants for sexual health, and abortion pills. Easy accessibility of these products in stores, pharmacies, and online platforms, without the need for a prescription, enabled them to conveniently manage their health. However, the ongoing debate and stigma surrounding self-managed abortion hindered decision-making.

Female college graduates shared their perspectives on menstrual health and hygiene practices with a particular emphasis on stigma, knowledge, accessibility, and preference for certain menstrual products. They shared that some people may face stigma for being conscientious about reproductive health matters. Participants also discussed factors contributing to a lack of knowledge and awareness regarding menstrual products and their proper usage. Additionally, they expressed feeling hesitant to try new products due to uncertainty about their ingredients and how to use them correctly. One of the participants, a 26-year-old female with unidentified sexuality, said, *"New products are hypoallergenic. We are demotivated because we lack knowledge and are unaware of their ingredients and how to use them correctly."* They, therefore, preferred using pads and tampons due to their easy accessibility and familiarity. Their preference was influenced by cultural norms, product availability, cost, and personal comfort.

"Pads and tampons are my go-to. They are easily accessible and are generally used."

A 24-year-old sexually active college graduate

"I haven't had a regular period for the last seven years. I use panty liners or tampons

as they cost less. My parents supported me when I started to use them."

A 26-year-old sexually active female bisexual

"During my period, whenever I needed a tampon, I would have to hide it. My periods have been weird."

A 23-year-old sexually active female pansexual

Participants shared their preferences for self-care products like self-injectables because of their convenience and comfort. A bisexual MBBS student said *"We do not want to see a gynecologist; we feel more comfortable injecting ourselves".*

Abortion

Personal experiences shared by college graduates revealed instances of unintended pregnancy. College graduates lacked knowledge about abortion. Birth control was generally accepted, but opinions on abortion varied, with some individuals viewing it as acceptable only in certain circumstances, such as during the beginning of sexual activity. There was a concern about the safety of self-induced abortion and about access to safe abortion services.

"Birth control is fine; I have no problem with it. Abortion, I think, is okay during the beginning of sexual activity. Family planning is very important. I don't think someone should have a child just because their parents made the decision. Yes, I will consult a doctor if the situation warrants it."

A 23-year-old sexually active single heterosexual male

"It's a very complicated subject, and there are a lot of things that people don't know about. I don't really know enough about it. I need to do more research. Yes, I will consult my parents and a doctor."

A 23-year-old sexually inactive male heterosexual

Young people emphasized the importance of support networks in overcoming demotivating factors related to reproductive health. Taboos within families can hinder access to resources, and they may, therefore, prefer to consult the medical system rather than their parents initially when facing reproductive health issues. One gay participant shared, *"there can be demotivating factors as they are not getting support or don't have the knowledge. It is considered a taboo in their families. In a way, taking them down."*

"I guess we would go to the medical system first because we trust it the most. We generally avoid talking to our parents first."

A 23-year-old sexually active male heterosexual

Practicing self-abortion can lead to complications.

"I don't think that it is safe at all. I am not motivated to do it on my own. I know a lot of women lack access to resources. Abortion is a huge thing. Having access to safe abortion is really important. It is very common for women to come in with excess vaginal bleeding because they tried to abort themselves. A lot of information is given to patients of vasectomy and tubectomy at the government hospital. Mostly we saw people coming for abortion directly."

29-year-old bisexual MBBS student

Source of information and knowledge

The study showed that college graduates understand the importance of knowing about certain SRH practices that can keep them safe and healthy. College graduates had different levels of awareness regarding self-care interventions for SRH, including contraception methods such as condoms, diaphragms, birth control pills, hormonal implants (e.g., nexplanon), and intrauterine devices (IUDs). On average, college graduates were aware of at least three to four contraceptive methods.

"It is very important to know about certain practices. It has helped me to know how to keep myself healthy and safe."

A 23-year-old sexually active male college graduate

"I know about the pill, the shot, the IUD, the arm implant, and barrier methods like the condom and diaphragm. Some people think pulling out is a form of birth control, and I guess for some people, this is a way of preventing pregnancy."

A 23-year-old sexually active female college graduate

College graduates received information on self-care interventions from schools, media, peers, older siblings, and healthcare providers. This diverse array of sources played a significant role in reducing the stigma associated with the use of contraceptives. Awareness was primarily due to their exposure to the right information in middle school or high school. *"Pills and Cu-T are used to prevent unwanted pregnancies. There are special sessions on sexual education in the school curriculum in Grade 8 and 9"* said a 29-year-old gay post-graduate student.

"I am aware of physical contraceptives like condoms, IUDs, birth control pills, the thing that gets in your arm, abstinence, and other methods. I learned about these things through my public schooling system in high school and middle school."

A 25-year-old sexually active male post-graduate student

"I am aware of the nexplanon implant, IUD, hormonal patch, birth control pills, condoms, and the pull-out method. I think I got this information through the media.

A 25-year-old queer female

Religious and cultural teachings impacted the level of awareness regarding SRH among college graduates from similar age groups. College graduates who studied at Catholic schools mentioned that they did not receive information through their schools. This shows that there are disparities in the quality and comprehensiveness of sex education in religious and conservative environments.

"I missed the memo on intercourse during middle school when everyone else in my school knew. So, I learned mostly from other middle school boys who could tell me things. I would then go and look things up on my own. In high school, there were health classes. I went to a private all boys school so I think that affected my understanding because they didn't tell us about contraceptives. It was a Catholic school, and it focused on abstinence. That class was kinda a joke, an easy A, and when I was 14, 15 that wasn't a priority."
A 23-year-old sexually active male heterosexual medical graduate student

"There's the shot, the pill, IUDs, nexplanon that goes in your arm, and condoms. I know there's plan B and I guess there's a pull-out method but I don't really think that counts, I don't agree. I think it's a risky method. I just had to research on my own or through talking to my peers. My high school focused on abstinence. I did not learn about SRH through school classes. It was mostly through talking to people of my age or undertaking personal research."
A 22-year-old female medical student.

Educational initiatives, other than the school curricula, were government programs, NGO campaigns, discussions among peers/friends and siblings, healthcare service providers, and online sources such as social media. These were the primary means for accessing adequate and appropriate information about SRH and self-care interventions. Understanding SRH was mentioned as beneficial for promoting healthy sexual behaviors and informed decision-making.

"There are a lot of foundations that are working on safe sexual practices. School curricula provide general guidelines to be followed."
A 29-year-old gay post-graduate student

"I got to know about contraceptives from social media, honestly. Now, when I think about it, it was in high and middle school. It is embarrassing that I didn't know about it till the age 17, 18, or maybe 19. I knew what the pill was but didn't know about so many other types of contraceptives like the IUD, patches, pills, shots. I

didn't know about the complexities of those until I got a job last year in healthcare. I learned in college through female friends and then saw patients with different contraceptive methods. So that was how I found out and now I know about a lot of different kinds."

A 23-year-old sexually active male heterosexual medical college graduate

While participants acknowledged the value of online sources for SRH information, they preferred to consult healthcare professionals. A college graduate mentioned, *"It is important to access SRH information online, but doctors should be the first ones to consult."* Planned Parenthood's informative website and resources such as "The Vagina Bible" were cited as valuable sources of information for individuals seeking guidance on SRH matters. However, they emphasized the need to critically evaluate online sources and prioritize information from reputable sources.

"Planned Parenthood has an informative website. If I don't know what to do, I use the book called 'The Vagina Bible' written by a gynecologist and it's helpful so when I'm like 'oh! what's happening here' or when I don't know something I read that."

A 23-year-old sexually active female graduate student

"My girlfriend did not get her period for the past two months. We both got pregnancy tests and consulted a doctor. It was depression that caused a delay in my period. Ultimately, it was resolved and it worked out."

A 25-year-old sexually active male heterosexual

Challenges and barriers

Social and cultural barriers

College graduates felt privileged that they could access SRH services without encountering stigma or discrimination. However, they noted that this privilege was influenced by sociocultural factors. For example, one participant from the queer community mentioned feeling privileged because she was white, which resulted in her encountering less stigma and other barriers in accessing SRH services. This was attributed partly to better socioeconomic status, education level, and social support networks. Another participant from a Hispanic background mentioned experiencing stigma at home regarding discussions about SRH, as premarital sex was considered a sin.

"I am a privileged white person so a lot of the other barriers weren't there. I never felt stigma or discrimination while getting services."

A 25-year-old queer female

"Sex could be really cultural. My partner and I belong to a Hispanic family... Mexicans and Americans face a lot of stigma...we both noticed that our parents are different...like his parents talked about sex but my mom did not. For my parents, sex before marriage is not advisable...nor is birth control."

A 24-year-old sexually active female college graduate

Similar experiences were shared by three other college graduates who attended Catholic schools. These institutions were not adept at discussing sexual health. However, it is important to note that these experiences were not universal among college graduates.

"I went to a Catholic school, and they weren't good at addressing sex education. I learned this stuff in middle school prior to high school."

A 25-year-old queer female

College graduates faced stigma from families and societies while communicating about sexual health. Their families did not feel comfortable discussing sexual matters with them. Parents felt hesitant to share information and to discuss sexual matters with them. They received information from their friends or from older siblings.

"I am not comfortable talking to my mother about sexual health. I spoke to my older siblings, who guided me."

A 20-year-old sexually active female graduate

"In school, professors really gave a lot of information. I wish my family would also. But there was and there still is stigma. I can talk to my mom about it. Teachers in elementary school told us about an at home pregnancy test. A friend showed it to me. I read the guidelines. They are actually effective and provide information within a short time about whether or not you're pregnant."

A 26-year-old female post-graduate student with unidentified sexuality

"Yes, I mean I know different types of birth control. I talk to my older siblings about safe sex, and we discuss our experiences. I also talk to my friends and to my sister."

A 20-year-old sexually active female graduate student

"I get a little embarrassed when I buy tampons or condoms at the store."

A 23-year-old sexually active female, pansexual college graduate

Other challenges

College graduates had a broad understanding of SRH issues. However, many faced systemic barriers in accessing SRH care. The study revealed that they faced financial constraints due to high costs, lack of insurance coverage, need for a prescription, and discrimination at healthcare facilities based on gender identity and sexual orientation.

"Self-care can feel like a privilege. Teaching is my hobby. In the US, formal healthcare is so expensive. I think that self-care practices should be treated as a privilege so that everyone has access to them."

A 24-year-old sexually active female college graduate

"There is a cost of obtaining any contraceptive or menstrual product. This is a

financial burden. We have to have a monthly budget."

A 25-year-old sexually active male heterosexual

Financial constraints significantly impacted decision-making and prioritizing sexual health. The study emphasized the importance of health insurance, particularly in places where healthcare costs were high.

"STI, it was mild. I probably could have taken an STI test but I didn't have university insurance. You have to pay yourself and I couldn't pay out-of-pocket. My insurance could have covered it but they didn't have any office in my location. There was some charge for it when I looked online. I could be wrong. I also worked at a sub-health center (SHC), but it was extremely confusing. Also, my parents could see that the charge was made from my student account. Mom would have suggested going to urgent care instead."

A 26-year-old sexually active female bisexual college graduate

College graduates faced challenges in accessing certain contraceptive methods due to the need of prescriptions. Prescription requirements posed a barrier to timely access to emergency contraception, particularly for individuals who did not have easy access to healthcare services. A 29-year-old bisexual female MBBS student mentioned, *"I am aware of contraceptives such as Plan B pill or I pill, Saheli (non-steroidal contraceptive for each cycle), but you need a prescription in the US now."* This limited accessibility and deterred individuals from obtaining contraceptives.

"I grew up in a small town. There was only one store there. So, I felt awkward buying there, so I ordered online from Amazon."

A 25-year-old sexually active male heterosexual college graduate

Experiences of a pansexual female and a bisexual non-binary with healthcare professionals were disappointing. They expressed feeling unsafe and judged based on their sexual preferences during the consultations, which exacerbated the stigma they already faced. Bisexual participants said that there were misconceptions among healthcare providers. They lacked training and did not understand equity and inclusivity in SRH care.

"Doctors wanted to put me on hormones. Now, I get them twice a month, and it's something I think about a lot as I have to deal with doctors. Doctors give weird answers and tell me things I don't want to hear. They tell me that I am unlucky because I am brown. That's not a diagnosis. I did actually get an IUD with someone's help when I was young. Planned Parenthood had a free option. If I take it out before a year, I would have to pay $2,000, I had to keep it in and suffer. I haven't found a system that works better for me. When I was young, my mom didn't believe in contraception so I had to do it alone. I was 15-16."

A 23-year-old sexually active pansexual female college graduate

"Primary care outside of Planned Parenthood for SRH has been mixed. There are many misconceptions among doctors who aren't well trained to think about equity and all. I wouldn't say I felt unsafe to access healthcare because I am financially pretty fortunate. But assumptions are made about me...about who I am involved with romantically or sexually."

A 26-year-old sexually active non-binary bisexual college graduate

Addressing these challenges requires providing comprehensive sexual education, improving healthcare access, and removing barriers that prevent equitable access to SRH services for young people.

Advancement of self-care

The study underscored the complex interplay of social, economic, and health related factors that affected the use of self-care interventions by college graduates. Early educational initiatives played a vital role in destigmatizing issues related to SRH. The main sources of knowledge about contraceptives were schools and colleges and online. However, decisions on how to use contraceptives and which ones to use were often made after discussions with peers and siblings.

College graduates shared their perspectives and experiences regarding the use of birth control pills and over-the-counter emergency contraception. They shared that peers and clinic representatives played a significant role in influencing decisions to use birth control pills. Discussion with peers about the availability and effectiveness of birth control pills motivated individuals to use them. Knowledge about their easy accessibility and availability influenced decision-making. Some participants shared their concerns about their unwillingness to use contraceptives and the stigma associated with them.

"A key motivator for considering the use of birth control pills involves discussions with peers and clinic representatives who provide information on their availability and effectiveness. Questions arise regarding why some individuals do not utilize them. Factors such as knowledge, accessibility, availability, costs, and insurance coverage affect their use. Additionally, there is the question of a prescription for some products."

A 26-year-old female post-graduate student with unidentified sexuality

"It can make your period more inconsistent, leading to irregularity...and has some medical risks in my experience."

A 24-year-old sexually active female college graduate

A supportive environment was provided by universities to promote SRH awareness and services. Resources made available through universities included information on STIs, methods of prevention, and free testing services. One postgraduate student said *"I had the benefit of the resources I needed. I had the support of my friends. I had access to resources from the university which helped me to gain confidence, and to navigate the problems."*

Institutions that facilitate easier access and raise awareness through discussions about STIs make it easier for college graduates. *"How can you be sure that you can have good SH? You should get your vitals checked. There are counters at the hospital where they talk about SRH and provide free testing for STIs. Normalizing discussions around STIs and promoting testing helps in reducing stigma and encourages individuals to take proactive steps to improve their sexual health."*

Although schools and universities are undertaking programs to inform youth about safe sexual practices, there are very few resources to inform them about how to educate themselves. There is, therefore, a need to educate youth on how they can educate themselves.

"The big thing is to educate people and to encourage them to educate themselves."
A 23-year-old non-active male heterosexual college graduate

The study suggests that self-care should be integrated within primary health care so that there is a greater emphasis on physical, mental, and social health rather than solely on chronic illnesses. Young adults, post-graduate students, and LGBTQ+ individuals exhibited distinct preferences for accessing SRH resources.

"The best way is to integrate self-care into primary health care, especially for those who belong to lower income backgrounds and have less access such as those who cannot see a doctor. Self-care should be emphasized and people should find ways to promote health. Doctors should focus on patients' mental health and social health."
A 23-year-old sexually active male heterosexual medical college graduate

As safety is paramount, community support is needed to facilitate access to self-care interventions. Healthcare providers, family, and peers can help individuals feel more comfortable while seeking reproductive health services. *"Safety is the most important factor—a leading factor that can help people access services and help them feel comfortable in using the services. People may not feel supported. The facility may not be easily accessible. There should be an inclusive network of doctors, family, and others to feel supported."*

Although knowledge builds confidence and erases stigma, affordability, and accessibility encourage college graduates to access essential products for self-management. If SRH is covered under insurance, it will motivate college graduates to access these services as high costs create a financial burden for individuals who are managing their finances. One of the participants mentioned, "*One should be able to get it at an accessible price. STI testing kits should be made available to all. Barriers should be minimized. Like if there are centers that provide services without identification. Education is important because people don't know how infection is transmitted.*"

"*The least motivating factor is cost. Stigma is attached to purchasing contraceptives. Public and non-religious universities are trying to make it less judgmental. My university has a policy like 'no questions asked'.*"

A 24-year-old sexually active female college graduate

A proactive approach is needed to manage the problem. It is important to have open discussions about safe-sex practices with doctors at healthcare centers. There should be flexibility in choosing healthcare providers.

"*It is important to know about day-to-day self-care. Doctors should be available at healthcare centers and should be accessible. We should also be able to change doctors if we want. And we should also be able to discuss sex practices openly.*"

Self-care and the COVID-19 factor

Restrictions during the pandemic impacted the daily lives of college graduates. They faced several challenges to maintain normalcy during the lockdowns. The supply chain was disrupted, and accessibility of certain items was affected. Limited mobility further exacerbated difficulties in accessing essential products. Experience shared by one of the participants highlighted that there was limited mobility and lack of access to necessary supplies. "*The stocks used to get over because everyone was trying to hoard. There were problems in accessing certain products as they were out of stock. We had to take several precautions. We had to sanitize and wear masks. How can you support yourself when you cannot go out?"*

The study showed that during the pandemic period there was uncertainty and vulnerability. College graduates sought safety through community and family support during that time. This had implications for their mental health. *"The pandemic impacted me to some degree, but it is hard to say how."* They adopted personal coping strategies during the pandemic. Universities played a proactive role in ensuring the wellbeing of their students. Institutional support during that period was crucial but insufficient. This led to challenges in overcoming mental health problems.

"Initially, we were trying to cope. We felt vulnerable. It was definitely a period when we wanted to feel safe. The university was a place where students could access information. Uncertainty affected mental health. Social media was another helpful source of information. But it was not the right source for me. People adopted their own ways in coping with the crisis"

A 29-year-old gay post-graduate student

While dealing with the pandemic, college graduates adapted to new realities and engaged in practicing self-care.

Self-care for sexual and reproductive health and rights through a gender lens

Regardless of gender, college graduates took complete responsibility for their SRH and were mindful when it came to their partner's SRH. However, when they recounted their experiences during their high school years when they first became sexually active, boys relied mainly on friends, while girls relied on older siblings and cousins for information on SRH and contraception. Individuals with other sexual preferences were well aware of safe sex practices.

Knowledge about self-care made the participants feel empowered. However, females using birth control pills or the hormonal IUD mentioned that it was inconvenient.

"Yes, for family planning, my girlfriend's input matters. But for the most part, it's just me. However, anything related to sexual health is a two-way thing with me and my girlfriend."
A 23-year-old sexually active male heterosexual medical college graduate

In most cases, college graduates decided mutually with their partners regarding sexual health matters and were willing to care for their partner's SRH. However, they often felt that women took greater responsibility due to the nature of birth control methods.

"Yes, mostly because of how contraceptives work in America; it is more on the woman than on the guy because she has to take a pill every day. We use condoms too but we don't have to remember to take a pill every day. Previously, my girlfriend had a hormonal IUD but she had it removed because it was affecting her health negatively. It really affected her and made her sad. This has been on my mind, too, because she recently said that she wanted to get an IUD again but a non-hormonal one. I need to do more research about it. I haven't really looked it up, but I've heard there are risks with that, too."
A 23-year-old sexually active male heterosexual medical graduate

"I think self-care is very important. I would also like to take care of my partner's SRH. Yes, I am aware of some hormonal tests, but I have never taken them."
A 29-year-old gay post-graduate student

"I learned everything through medical study. I know the causes and the treatment of STIs. I also know about other diseases. So, I guess that to understand how STI happens...it is at the time when sex fluids are exchanged. The disease can be transmitted through these fluids. Unless you are with one partner you should definitely take all precautions. It is always good to use condoms, especially if you have anal sex, because the probability of transferring the disease is higher. While

having oral sex, like during blow jobs, infectious diseases can be transmitted."

A 29-year-old bisexual MBBS student

Students felt empowered with self-care practices. *"I would recommend it; I feel empowered."*

Discussion

In the US, approximately 22 percent of the population comprises young people who are 15-19 years old; 21 percent are 20-25 years of age (54). In this young population, 79 percent of females and 77 percent of males aged 15-24 are sexually active by the age of 20. Studies show that 15-19 years old adolescents are most vulnerable to sexual health related problems and are at higher risk of unwanted pregnancy. Although the data shows a decline in early pregnancies by 72 percent from its peak in 1991, this number is still very high when compared to other developed countries, as reported by the National Survey of Family Growth (NSFG) 2015-2017. The reasons for this decline are not totally clear. Some reported reasons to include abstaining from sexual activity and using birth control (55). Contraceptive use is influenced by women's knowledge, beliefs, and perceptions of contraceptive side-effects and health risks, as well as by educational programs run by the US government. These educational initiatives include sexuality education programs, youth development programs, abstinence education programs, clinic-based programs, and programs specifically designed for diverse populations in different settings. This could be the possible reason for the change in attitude among females (55)(56). Educational initiatives also cover other topics as mentioned in the report by Planned Parenthood. Those are sex education, STIs, puberty, healthy relationships, birth control, and sexual orientation.

Research indicates that college graduates above the age of 19 in the US prioritize their sexual and reproductive health irrespective of their gender. Young people generally practice self-care and have a good understanding of how to promote SRH. College graduates are aware of several contraceptive methods and know how to use them. However, this knowledge varies based on age, ethnicity, sexual orientation, and experience of engaging with multiple partners. There has been an increase in knowledge among youth of various self-care interventions. The primary sources of information are educational institutions, mainly middle and high schools, and online platforms. For the current generation, online platforms serve as the main source of information for self-care interventions. However, obtaining reliable information online remains challenging. According to research conducted by the Berkeley School of Information, more than 97 percent of teens use the internet daily. Adolescents turn to social media sites for advice and information. However, these platforms often provide misinformation, which poses a serious threat (57).

Our study indicates that young people are aware of the importance of SRH. However, they lack practical details on how to use contraceptives correctly. Decisions are mostly made through discussions with peers and elder siblings. There are disparities in knowledge because Catholic schools provide limited education. College graduates learn through self-education and with the help of peers and friends or access information online. However, there is often a delay in accessing information, which can lead to problems.

The research study provides insights into the attitudes and behaviors of college graduates and their experiences with accessing SRH services. Condom is the most commonly used contraceptive method. Condoms offer dual protection against pregnancy and STIs. Condom use is perceived as an empowering factor. The second most commonly used contraceptive is birth control pills (58). However, there are concerns about their side-effects.

Contraceptive use among female teenagers (15 to 19 years old) increased in 2017-2019 as compared to 2002 (59). The use of condoms increased from 93.7 percent to 95.4 percent in 2015-2019. There was an increase in the withdrawal method from 55 percent to 64.8 percent. There was a huge increase in IUD usage from 0.2 percent to 6.1 percent and in the use of the implant from 0.1 percent to 13.3 percent. The use of emergency contraception increased from 8.1 percent to 22.3 percent. However, the use of birth control pills has decreased from 61.4 percent to 52 percent over the last 15 to 18 years (59). Only 38.7 percent of individuals aged 15 to 19 use oral contraceptive pills. In contrast, the rate of using any contraceptive method increased to 60.9 percent among those aged 20 to 29. This data is indicative of a change in sexual attitudes towards the use of contraceptives among these age groups, which is representative of young people in the US (60). Our research study corroborated these findings, suggesting that practicing self-care is a means of preventing pregnancy among young people in the age group of 15 to 23 years. Graduates 23 years of age and above also use contraceptives to prevent STIs.

College graduates access self-testing kits mainly through pharmacies. These include pregnancy test kits, HIV and HPV self-testing kits, and other STIs self-testing kits. But they are concerned about the accuracy of these self-testing methods. Self-testing is cost-effective and helps to overcome barriers that prevent in-person encounters and thus prevent youth from facing stigma at healthcare centers. By increasing privacy, confidentiality, and anonymity, self-testing addresses the problem of stigma and discrimination, which prevents people from seeking in-person HIV testing (50).

There are barriers to self-managing abortion. These are due to societal attitudes which make individuals hesitant to seek information or engage in discussion. The study revealed that there is a clear knowledge gap regarding available menstrual products and their correct usage. This also raises concerns about managing serious procedures such as abortion.

The research study underscored several challenges and suggested that to overcome these challenges, self-care must be promoted. It emphasized the effect of socioeconomic status, race, education level, and social support networks on SRH outcomes. White Americans tend to experience greater privilege in accessing SRH services. Conversely, individuals from Hispanic and Catholic backgrounds face stigma and barriers when discussing SRH within their families. Some groups also encounter discomfort in purchasing essential SRH products like tampons and condoms. A study conducted by Brown et al. in the US highlights the impact of various socioeconomic and cultural factors on contraceptive use and unintended pregnancy (18).

Financial constraints and discrimination based on gender identity and sexual orientation also hinder accessibility. Our study shows that self-care was considered a privilege. However, financial barriers inhibited reproductive autonomy. A study undertaken in 2023 shows how burdensome costs can be in accessing SRH care. People postpone seeking SRH care due to cost barriers (61).

Our study highlights the significance of self-care from a gender perspective. It is important to create a space for discussion on contraceptive choices involving considerations of their effectiveness and their impacts on health. Mutual decision-making with partners is considered important for managing SRH problems.

The research findings underscore the importance of personalized self-care practices, including nutrition, exercise, and quality time with loved ones, for achieving overall wellbeing. However, concerns were raised regarding the commercialization of self-care, which has transformed into a booming industry. Relying on new methods of self-care can be costly, as highlighted in a 2018 Harvard Business Review article, which indicates that there is a shift in focus from holistic self-care to a more technology-driven approach (62). Another motivational factor is accessible healthcare facilities, pharmacies, and health centers. There is a need to increase the sources of information by providing an educational platform for SRHR and enabling open discussions on safe sex and contraception. Universities play an important role in promoting SRH practices. Efforts should be made to destigmatize STIs and provide free testing services. Supportive networks are vital for making individuals feel safe and comfortable. This support is crucial for overcoming barriers related to stigma and accessibility.

Concluding comments

Our research sheds light on the attitudes, behaviors, and practices of young people regarding their sexual and reproductive health. The landscape for SRH practices among young adults in the US is complex. While there has been a notable decline in early pregnancies over the past few decades, challenges persist among adolescents 15 and 19 years of age. They remain vulnerable to SRH-related problems. It is important for middle and high schools to provide SRH information. Experience of unwanted pregnancy as a result of engaging in risky sexual practices highlights the need for more research to assess the effectiveness of educational programs and the reach of existing resources for high school students in the age group of 15 to 19 years.

Educational institutions and media platforms are key sources of information on SRH. Providing information related to SRH in middle and high schools is crucial. However, Catholic schools in the US do not provide this information. Therefore, young people lack information on the use of contraceptives and SRH products. There are disparities in SRH information among young people, especially in underserved areas. Hispanic Americans and Catholics face stigma and socioeconomic barriers in accessing SRH services. Schools are required to incorporate comprehensive sexual health education in their curricula to cover contraceptives and provide practical guidance on their use. Efforts should be made to advance SRH services in underserved areas. It is also important to make SRH services affordable for all.

Our study underscores the need to enable young people in the US to adopt a holistic approach to self-care that integrates physical, mental, and social health practices. However, the commercialization of self-care has impacted its affordability and accessibility, particularly for people in underserved areas and marginalized communities.

Further research should explore the relationship between stigma, environmental consciousness, and attitudes toward reproductive health practices among diverse populations. Public health campaigns should focus on destigmatizing discussions on sexual and reproductive health matters. They should foster a supportive environment where individuals feel comfortable and safe to discuss these matters and to seek information and services. Research should be undertaken to investigate the role of education and information campaigns in promoting awareness and acceptance of new menstrual products, particularly for populations with limited access to reproductive health services. It is also important to understand the factors driving individual preferences for specific menstrual products and how accessibility impacts their choices especially in regions with limited access to menstrual products. There is also a need to generate awareness about the environmental impact of menstrual products. Additionally, it is important to explore people's attitudes and behaviors towards eco-friendly alternatives and to identify the barriers that prevent them from adopting these sustainable options.

Research should explore the impact of social support and cultural norms on individuals' reproductive health decisions and behaviors. Strategies for reducing financial and logistical barriers to reproductive health services should be implemented. Research should be undertaken to understand the factors that influence individual preferences for self-administered contraceptives and other self-care interventions.

Acknowledgments

The authors thank Samuel C. Okorie and Meda Hope Malinga, Youth Mentor and Ambassador for Africa at the POP Movement, Aishwarya Rao, and Mackenzie Stoeltje, students at New York University, for interviewing participants in the United States and for providing support in reaching the targeted groups included in the study. We appreciate their support for this research endeavor.

References

1. Abdurahman C, Oljira L, Hailu S & Mengesha MM. Sexual and reproductive health services utilization and associated factors among adolescents attending secondary schools. Reproductive Health. 2022 Jul 15; 19:161. https://www.ncbi.nlm.nih.gov/pmc/articles/PMC9287868/

2. Sedgh G & Sorhaindo A. Identifying and prioritizing evidence needs in self-care interventions for sexual and reproductive health. Frontier Global Womens Health. 2023 Jun 8;4. https://www.frontiersin.org/journals/global-womens-health/articles/10.3389/fgwh.2023.1148244/full

3. World Health Organization. WHO consolidated guideline on self-care interventions for health. World Health Organization https://iris.who.int/bitstream/handle/10665/325480/9789241550550-eng.pdf?ua=1

4. UNICEF. Adolescent health dashboard regional profiles. UNICEF. 2023 Jun. https://data.unicef.org/resources/adolescent-health-dashboard-regional-profiles/

5. Guttmacher Institute. Unintended pregnancy in the United States. Guttmacher Institute. 2019 Jan. https://www.guttmacher.org/sites/default/files/factsheet/fb-unintended-pregnancy-us_0_4.pdf

6. Statista. Age distribution in the United States from 2012 to 2022. Statista, United States. 2024. https://www.statista.com/statistics/270000/age-distribution-in-the-united-states/

7. American Psychological Association. Risky Business: Curbing adolescent sexual behaviors with interventions. American Psychological Association. 2006 Sep 15. https://www.apa.org/topics/sex-sexuality/high-risk-behavior-adolescents

8. Srahbzu M & Tirfeneh E. Risky sexual behavior and associated factors among adolescents aged 15-19 years at Governmental High Schools in Aksum Town, Tigray, Ethiopia, 2019: An institution-based, cross-sectional study. Biochemistry Research International. 2020 Aug 21;2020:3719845. https://www.ncbi.nlm.nih.gov/pmc/articles/PMC7456495/

9. World Health Organization. Programming for adolescent health and development. Report of a WHO/UNFPA/UNICEF Study Group. World Health

Organization. 1999 Mar 25;(886): 1–260. https://www.who.int/publication s/i/item/9241208864

10. Center for Disease Control. Youth engage in sexual risk behaviors. Adolescent and School Health, Center for Disease Control. 2024 Mar 26. https://www.cdc.gov/healthyyouth/sexualbehaviors/index.htm

11. Lindberg LD, Firestein L & Beavin C. Trends in U.S. Adolescent sexual behavior and contraceptive use, 2006-2019. Contraception: X. 2021 Jan 1;3:100064. https://www.sciencedirect.com/science/article/pii/S25901516 21000113

12. YRBS. Youth Risk Behavior Survey Data Summary & Trends Report: 2011-2021. Youth.Gov. 2023 Feb 13. https://youth.gov/feature-article/2011-2021-yrbs-data-summary-and-trends-report

13. Madeline H-K. Binge drinking: Effects, risks, and dangers of binge drinking. American Addiction Centers. 2024 Aug 16. https://americanaddicti oncenters.org/alcohol/binge-drinking

14. American Addiction Centers. Substance abuse statistics among young adults. American Addiction Centers. 2024 Apr 4. https://americanaddictionc enters.org/addiction-statistics/young-adults

15. AACAP. Teens: Alcohol and other drugs. American Academy of Child & Adolescent Psychiatry. 2018 Mar. https://www.aacap.org/AACAP/Families _and_Youth/Facts_for_Families/FFF-Guide/Teens-Alcohol-And-Other-rugs-003.aspx

16. Cho HS & Yang Y. Relationship between alcohol consumption and risky sexual behaviors among adolescents and young adults: A meta-analysis. International Journal of Public Health. 2023 Apr 19; 68:1605669. https://ww w.ncbi.nlm.nih.gov/pmc/articles/PMC10154531/

17. Centers for Disease Control. Substance use and sexual risk behaviors among teens. Adolescent and School Health. CDC. 2019. https://www.cdc.go v/healthyyouth/factsheets/substance_use_fact_sheet-basic.htm

18. Institute of Medicine (US) Committee on Unintended Pregnancy; Brown SS, Eisenberg L, editors. Socioeconomic and cultural influences on contraceptive use in The best intentions: Unintended pregnancy and the well-being of children and families. NCBI Bookshelf. National Academic Press.

1995. https://www.ncbi.nlm.nih.gov/books/NBK232120/

19. Guttmacher Institute. Unintended pregnancy in the United States. Guttmacher Institute. https://www.guttmacher.org/sites/default/files/fact sheet/fb-unintended-pregnancy-us_0_4.pdf

20. Statista. Population by race in the U.S. 2022. Statista. https://www.statista.com/statistics/183489/population-of-the-us-by-ethnicity-since-2000/

21. Miller MK, Wickliffe J, Jahnke S, Linebarger JS & Dowd D. Accessing general and sexual healthcare: Experiences of urban youth. Vulnerable Child Youth Study. 2014 Jul 1;9(3):279–90. https://www.ncbi.nlm.nih.gov/pmc/articles/PMC4119761/

22. FindLaw Staff. State-by-state marriage "age of consent" laws. 2023 Jun 29. FindLaw https://www.findlaw.com/family/marriage/state-by-state -marriage-age-of-consent-laws.html

23. AgeOfConsent. United States age of consent laws by state. AgeOfConsent. https://www.ageofconsent.net/states

24. Craig AD, Dehlendorf C, Borrero S, Harper CC & Rocca CH. Exploring young adults' contraceptive knowledge and attitudes: disparities by race/ethnicity and age. Womens Health Issues Official Publication of the Jacobs Institute Women's Health. 2014; 24(3): e281–289. https://www.ncbi.nlm.nih.gov/pmc/articles/PMC4119871/

25. Witwer E., Jones R.K., & Lindberg l.D. Sexual behavior and contraceptive and condom use among U.S. high school students, 2013–2017. Guttmacher Institute. 2018 Sep. https://www.guttmacher.org/report/sexual-behavior-contraceptive-condom-use-us-high-school-students-2013-2017

26. Sadler L.S., Dynes M.W., Daley A.M., Ickovics J.R., Leventhal J.M. & Reynolds H. MSN. Use of home pregnancy tests among adolescent women. MCN: The American Journal of Maternal/Child Nursing. 2004 Jan; 29(1):50. https://journals.lww.com/mcnjournal/abstract/2004/01000/use_of_hom e_pregnancy_tests_among_adolescent_women.13.aspx

27. Sadler LS, Dynes MW, Daley AM, Ickovics JR, Leventhal JM, Reynolds H. Use of home pregnancy tests among adolescent women. MCN: The American Journal of Maternal/Child Nursing. 2004 Jan; 29(1):50. https://journals.lww

.com/mcnjournal/abstract/2004/01000/use_of_home_pregnancy_tests_among_adolescent_women.13.aspx

28. Guttmacher Institute. U.S. teenage pregnancies, births and abortions: National and state trends and trends by race and ethnicity. Guttmacher Institute. 2010 Jan. https://www.guttmacher.org/sites/default/files/pdfs/pubs/USTPtrends.pdf

29. Finer LB & Henshaw SK. Disparities in rates of unintended pregnancy in the United States, 1994 and 2001. Perspectives on Sexual and Reproductive Health. 2006 Jun;38(2):90–96. https://pubmed.ncbi.nlm.nih.gov/16772190/

30. Henshaw SK. Unintended pregnancy in the United States. Family Planning Perspective. 1998;30(1):24–9, 46. https://pubmed.ncbi.nlm.nih.gov/9494812/

31. Diamant J., Mohamed B., & Leppert R. What the data says about abortion in the U.S. Pew Research Center. 2024 Mar 25. https://www.pewresearch.org/short-reads/2024/03/25/what-the-data-says-about-abortion-in-the-us/

32. Romero L. Reduced disparities in birth rates among teens aged 15–19 years — United States, 2006–2007 and 2013–2014. Morbidity and Mortality Weekly Report. 2016;65. https://www.cdc.gov/mmwr/volumes/65/wr/mm6516a1.htm

33. Centers for Disease Control and Prevention. Trends in sexual risk behaviors among high school students—United States, 1991-1997. Morbidity and Mortality Weekly Report. 1998 Sep 18;47(36):749–52. https://pubmed.ncbi.nlm.nih.gov/9756456/

34. Brown LK, DiClemente R, Crosby R, Fernandez MI, Pugatch D, Cohn S, et al. Condom use among high-risk adolescents: Anticipation of partner disapproval and less pleasure associated with not using condoms. Public Health Reports. 2008;123(5):601–7. https://www.ncbi.nlm.nih.gov/pmc/articles/PMC2496933/

35. Thoma BC & Huebner DM. Parent-adolescent communication about sex and condom use among young men who have sex with men: An examination of the theory of planned behavior. Annals of Behavioral Medicine. 2018 Feb

27;52(11):973−87. https://www.ncbi.nlm.nih.gov/pmc/articles/PMC619636 6/

36. Jerman J, Onda T & Jones RK. What are people looking for when they Google "self-abortion"? Contraception. 2018 Jun 1;97(6):510−4. https://www.sciencedirect.com/science/article/pii/S0010782418300684

37. Verma N & Grossman D. Self-managed abortion in the United States. Current Obstetrics and Gynecology Reports. 2023;12(2):70−5. https://www.ncbi.nlm.nih.gov/pmc/articles/PMC9989574/

38. Rachel K. Jones. Medication abortion now accounts for more than half of all US abortions. Guttmacher Institute. 2022. https://www.guttmacher.org/article/2022/02/medication-abortion-now-accounts-more-half-all-us-abortions

39. Selena S-D. Despite bans in some states, more than a million abortions were provided in 2023. 2024 Mar 19. https://www.npr.org/sections/health-shots/2024/03/19/1238293143/abortion-data-how-many-us-2023

40. Sullivan B & Selena S-D. Beyond the "abortion pill": Real-life experiences of individuals taking mifepristone. NPR. 2024 Mar 26. https://www.npr.org/sections/health-shots/2023/05/17/1176514276/mifepristone-abortion-miscarriage-pill

41. Human Rights Watch. Human rights crisis: Abortion in the United States after Dobbs. Human Rights Watch. 2023 Apr 18. https://www.hrw.org/news/2023/04/18/human-rights-crisis-abortion-united-states-after-dobbs#_ftn2

42. Popinchalk A & Sedgh G. Trends in the method and gestational age of abortion in high-income countries. BMJ Sexual & Reproductive Health. 2019 Apr;45(2):95−103. Available from: https://jfprhc.bmj.com/lookup/doi/10.1136/bmjsrh-2018-200149

43. Guttmacher Institute. Many young women in the United States turn to google for information on self-abortion. Guttmacher Institute. 2018 Feb 26. https://www.guttmacher.org/news-release/2018/many-young-women-united-states-turn-google-information-self-abortion

44. ANSIRH. Availability of telehealth services for medication abortion in the U.S., 2020-2022. Advancing New Standards in Reproductive Health.

2023 Jun 20. https://www.ansirh.org/research/brief/availability-telehealth-services-medication-abortion-us-2020-2022

45. Society of Family Planning. #WeCount report April 2022 to June 2023. The Society of Family Planning. 2023 Oct 24. https://societyfp.org/wp-content/uploads/2023/10/WeCountReport_10.16.23.pdf

46. Keeter GP & Keeter S. At least four-in-ten U.S. adults have faced high levels of psychological distress during COVID-19 pandemic. Pew Research Center. 2022. https://www.pewresearch.org/short-reads/2022/12/12/at-least-four-in-ten-u-s-adults-have-faced-high-levels-of-psychological-distress-during-covid-19-pandemic/

47. Press A. US women stock up on abortion pills, especially when restrictions in news. Voice of America. 2024 Jan 02. https://www.voanews.com/a/us-women-stock-up-on-abortion-pills-especially-when-restrictions-in-news-/7421959.html

48. Coles MS, Makino KK, & Phelps R. Medication abortion knowledge among adolescent medicine providers. Journal of Adolescent Health. 2012 Apr;50(4):383–8. https://www.ncbi.nlm.nih.gov/pmc/articles/PMC3637969/

49. Centers for Disease Control and Prevention. Getting tested for HIV. Centers for Disease Control and Prevention. 2024. https://www.cdc.gov/hiv/testing/index.html

50. Centers for Disease Control and Prevention. Issue brief: The role of HIv self-testing in ending the HIV pandemic. Centers for Disease Control and Prevention. 2024 https://www.cdc.gov/hiv/policies/data/self-testing-issue-brief.html

51. Menza TW, Garai J, Ferrer J & Hecht J. Rapid uptake of home-based HIV self-testing during social distancing for SARS-CoV2 infection in Oregon. AIDS and Behavior. 2021;25(1):167–70. https://www.ncbi.nlm.nih.gov/pmc/articles/PMC7320648/

52. Freeman AE, Sullivan P, Higa D, Sharma A, MacGowan R, Hirshfield S, et al. Perceptions of HIV self-testing among men who have sex with men in the United States: A qualitative analysis. AIDS Education and Prevention: Official Publication of the International Society for AIDS Education. 2018

Feb;30(1):47−62. https://pubmed.ncbi.nlm.nih.gov/29481298/

53. Lippman SA, Moran L, Sevelius J, Castillo LS, Ventura A, Treves-Kagan S, et al. Acceptability and feasibility of HIV self-testing among transgender women in San Francisco: A mixed methods pilot study. AIDS and Behavior. 2016 Apr;20(4):928−38. https://pubmed.ncbi.nlm.nih.gov/26511864/

54. Korhonen V. Number of U.S. youth and young adult population by age 2022. Statista. 2024 Jul 05. https://www.statista.com/statistics/221852/number-of-youth-and-young-adult-population-in-the-us/

55. Centers for Disease Control and Prevention. About teen pregnancy. Centers for Disease Control and Prevention. Reproductive Health. 2024 https://www.cdc.gov/reproductive-health/teen-pregnancy/index.html

56. Planned Parenthood. What's the state of sex education in the U.S? Planned Parenthood. https://www.plannedparenthood.org/learn/for-educators/whats-state-sex-education-us

57. Berkeley School of Information. University of California researchers win grant to study misinformation surrounding reproductive health on social Media. Berkeley Research. 2023 Nov 16. https://vcresearch.berkeley.edu/news/university-california-researchers-win-grant-study-misinformation-surrounding-reproductive

58. Szucs LE. Condom and contraceptive use among sexually active high school students — Youth risk behavior survey, United States, 2019. Morbidity and Mortality Weekly Report, CDC. 2020 Aug 21;69. https://www.cdc.gov/mmwr/volumes/69/su/su6901a2.htm

59. National Center for Health Statistics. National health statistics reports, number 196. National Center for Health Statistics. 2023 Dec 14;(196). https://www.cdc.gov/nchs/nhis/nhis_nhsr.htm

60. Daniels K & Abma JC. Current contraceptive status among women aged 15-49: United Status, 2017-2019. National Center for Health Statistics. 2020 Oct. https://www.cdc.gov/nchs/products/databriefs/db388.htm

61. VandeVusse A, Hussain R, Stillman M, Beavin C, Kirstein M & Kavanaugh ML. Cost-related barriers to sexual and reproductive health care: Results from a longitudinal qualitative study in Arizona. SSM - Qualitative Research in Health. 2023 Dec 01;4:100360. https://www.sciencedirect.com/science/

article/pii/S2667321523001440

62. Lieberman C. How self-care became so much work. Harvard Business Review. 2018 Aug 10. https://hbr.org/2018/08/how-self-care-became-so-much-work

A Narrative of a 25-Year-Old Woman Navigating Sexual and Reproductive Health During the COVID-19 Pandemic

This is the story of a 25-year-old financially independent female college graduate living in Los Angeles, California. She worked in marketing and aspired to a more creative career path. She identified herself as 'queer' and prioritized personality over gender. She had a couple of sexual involvements but was currently single after a recent breakup.

She prioritized her health, practiced self-care, and knew how to go about it. Even during the pandemic, the kind of experiences she shared provided a clear picture of how a proactive attitude toward her health helped her overcome difficult situations and mental health issues. The pandemic proved to be a major transition year for her. She graduated in 2020 and started to live in a shared apartment with her roommates. Her life was significantly impacted during that time due to various reasons like weak finances, family dependency, shifting living places, and other relationship experiences. Initially, during the pandemic, she moved in with her parents due to differences she had with her roommates. She mentioned, "*At the start of the pandemic, I moved into my parent's house because my roommates used to bring people back home. I like to keep my bed clean and my room tidy. But my roommates were a little messier and always kept the house untidy.*"

After her breakup, she struggled with anxiety and depression that impacted her mental health. She said that she consumed *marijuana to cope with* her anxiety. She recalled, "My *marijuana use went through the roof, I adopted it heavily and continued it for long.*" Later, she moved into a studio apartment in Chicago and experienced social isolation. However, she coped through yoga, meditation, and binge-watching reality TV shows. She mentioned, "*I binge-watched reality television— TopChef, RuPaul, and Survivor and started doing yoga and meditation. I'm not into exercising generally. But yoga helped me cope with my mental health problems, and it was easy to stick with it.*" She highlighted the importance of support from friends and family, which was instrumental in navigating the pandemic's challenges. She began taking medication for anxiety in 2021, which improved her anxiety and communication difficulties, especially with her partner at that time. Soon after that, she started therapy. She faced many issues, but medication helped her clear the fog. Despite initial challenges in accessing the medicines, insurance proved to be beneficial.

She had comprehensive sexual and reproductive health knowledge. She attended a Catholic high school where limited sexual education was provided. However, she educated herself through the media, personal research, and friends. She said, "*I think I got this information through the media. I went to a Catholic school, and they were not good at addressing sexual education. I learned this myself in middle school.*" Despite her religious upbringing, she developed a sexually open and expressive outlook, primarily informed by personal research and experience rather than through formal education. She obtained information online, usually through mobile applications for medical information and by browsing credible sources such as articles. When asked how she assessed the integrity of the information online, she pleasantly recalls her personal experience, "*I am not sure, but I usually try to read the full article instead of just the headline. At first, when I got into a long-term relationship, I started using the hormonal patch because I thought I would forget to take the pill regularly, but the patch was inconvenient. I then switched to nexplanon which was given to me by my medical provider.*"

Not in any relationship right now, earlier she was sexually active with two partners. She was aware of safe sexual practices and the importance of communication to ensure mutual comfort and safety. She recounts safe sexual practices as *"things such as wearing a condom, using birth control, and communicating with your partner to ensure that the other feels safe and comfortable. I think communication is the key."* She mentioned obtaining information on birth control primarily through online resources. She has a positive attitude toward sexual health and family planning. She was well-informed about various contraceptive methods such as the nexplanon implant, IUDs, hormonal patches, birth control pills, condoms, and the pull-out method. She preferred long-term contraceptives and was using the nexplanon implant. Lack of support did not affect her SRH during the pandemic. She mentioned, *"No, because I have a long-term birth control implant, so it never really discontinued."*

Identifying herself as queer she had been facing several hormonal issues, specifically hormonal acne which got worse after she stopped birth control to regulate her hormones. She said, *"I have been having a bad bout of hormonal acne on my chin. I got off birth control to regularize my hormones. But yes, I have been having issues."*

She holds strong pro-choice views on birth control, family planning, and abortion and believes in the right to terminate pregnancy. When asked how important SRH is to her, she says *"Very important. I don't want children right now. Everyone needs to take the necessary precautions. I am young and do not have money to raise a child. All my partners are of similar age so we cannot take that responsibility."* She stressed the use of contraceptives, especially in preventing unplanned pregnancy, as she does not feel ready for children due to her current financial and professional situation. Her partners, being of similar age and mindset, also prioritize these precautions.

Reflecting on her experiences with SRH services, when it comes to self-care products, she used over-the-counter hormonal contraceptives and menstrual hygiene products like pads and tampons. She did not feel the need for emergency contraception, vaginal contraceptive rings, or self-administered contraception as she prefers using long-term contraceptive methods. She started using contraceptives at a very young age. She said, *"I got my implant through Kaiser when I was 20 and in a long-term relationship. It was easy to access."* As a white American, she felt privileged as she never had to face stigma while accessing any of the self-care products such as pregnancy tests, abortion pills, tampons, or condoms. She admits, *"I am a privileged white person, so there were no such barriers in accessing self-care products. I never felt stigma or discrimination for getting healthcare services."* She also mentioned, *"If I thought I was pregnant, I would certainly seek out pregnancy tests and abortion as I do not want children right now. There's no stigma related to buying tampons/condoms."* Even during the COVID-19 pandemic, her use of SRH services remained stable as she was already on long-term contraception. She did not face any SRH problems during the lockdown and did not experience stigma or discrimination while accessing services.

She was very proactive in maintaining her SRH. There were many instances when she shared her experiences of using preventive self-care interventions. For SRH conditions like urinary tract infections (UTIs), she accessed urgent healthcare. She underwent two PAP smears, including cervical screenings, and relied on condoms for protection against HIV and other sexually transmitted infections (STIs). She was aware of the importance of PrEP and of maintaining a low viral load for HIV-positive individuals. Cost did not impact her choices in SRH as her insurance covered these expenses.

"I have had four UTIs. I went to urgent care and had to pay out-of-pocket. I haven't had STIs but I have had UTIs. I ended up getting reimbursed. It's just an annoying extra step."

She preferred insured health treatment. She was aware of self-care interventions despite facing some challenges in accessing them. This was mainly due to health insurance limitations at the time such as location, health issues covered by insurance, appointments, waiting times, and reimbursements.

She faced challenges in accessing mental health therapy as well as STI tests, as her insurance did not cover those. However, she managed through urgent care visits and telehealth counseling. She mentioned, *"For my mental health issues, I knew I just wanted to go for telehealth where it was on and off. I got one referral through my mom's friend. However, it was challenging to get appointments because of insurance, waiting, and finding providers. But once I got through it, it was good. It's paid out-of-pocket. My mom is paying for it. I do have health insurance right now but I am changing it. I think my new insurance will cover therapy. It is through my job."*

Speaking of the advancement of self-care, she felt that being financially independent helped her make decisions. Additionally, the support she received from friends and partners helped her adopt self-care practices. She was a supporter of health insurance. *"I had support for these practices. I couldn't have gone through all those times without them [my friends]. Being with people was more important than self-care practice."*

Comparison of Self-Care Experiences Across Different Countries

Saroj Pachauri, Public Health Specialist, Trustee, Center for Human Progress, New Delhi, India, and Director, POP (Protect Our Planet) Movement, New York, USA

Ash Pachauri, Director, Center for Human Progress, New Delhi, India, and Senior Mentor, POP (Protect Our Planet) Movement, New York, USA

Drishya Pathak, Research Associate, Center for Human Progress, New Delhi, India and Youth Mentor, POP (Protect Our Planet) Movement, New York, USA

Komal Mittal, Research Associate, Center for Human Progress, New Delhi, India and Youth Mentor, POP (Protect Our Planet) Movement, New York, USA

Background

Currently, young people make up a significant portion of the global population (1). The United Nations estimates that by 2030 there will be around 1.3 billion people between the ages of 15 and 24 years. Every country has its own unique demographic makeup. The top 10 countries with the highest numbers of young people in the world are in Africa. Niger is the youngest country in the world with almost 50 percent of its population under the age of 15 years (2). Essential prerequisites for harnessing this demographic dividend are providing education and healthcare to youth.

As defined by the World Health Organization (WHO), self-care is the "*ability of individuals, families, and communities to promote health, prevent disease, maintain health, and cope with illness and disability with or without the support of a health worker"*. Self-care encompasses physical, mental, and emotional wellbeing. It includes self-awareness, happiness, readiness for change, and staying connected with friends, family, and the community. Self-care is different and unique for individuals depending on their needs and what they consider is important for their lives (3).

Currently, half of the world's population of around 3.6 billion people lacks access to essential health services. WHO recommends that in order to achieve Universal Health Coverage, it is important to implement self-care practices to promote health, ensure safety, and support the vulnerable (4).

Barriers to health services and self-care interventions among young people

Globally, there are one billion youth aged 15-24 years who faced challenges in accessing health services. Limited educational resources and a lack of access to digital health information make it challenging for young people to learn about their healthcare options. Even when healthcare is accessible, factors such as provider bias limit young people's ability to receive high-quality care (5).

Self-care interventions are evidence-based tools. They include medicines, diagnostic kits, and digital technologies that empower people to take charge of their own health. Self-care places people at the center and reduces pressure on the health system. For young people, embracing self-care is crucial. Taking care of oneself is essential. Self-care measures are not self-centered. Self-care interventions provide choices enabling young people the option to access healthcare wherever and whenever they want to (6).

Young leaders must be included in discussions on self-care. Their voices must be heard as self-care interventions are designed. By shifting the focus to young people's needs and ensuring they have the right knowledge and resources, we can work towards a future where all young person can manage their health effectively (5).

Comparison of self-care interventions across different countries

Data was collected from 2021 to 2023 from four countries: Mexico, India, the USA, and Nigeria. While undertaking a comparative data analysis, we identified common themes across all countries. We also observed country-specific themes unique to each country. Based on these findings, we outlined three primary domains for further analysis: 1) concerns about sexual and reproductive health and rights (SRHR); 2) perceptions and usage of self-care interventions for sexual and reproductive health (SRH); and 3) challenges for adopting self-care to improve SRH.

Concerns about sexual and reproductive health and rights

Understanding sexual and reproductive health and rights

High school students in Mexico, the USA, and Nigeria had some understanding of safe sexual practices, including oral, vaginal, and anal sex. High school students in India had little to no knowledge about these sexual practices. In all four countries, older people aged 19 to 26 years, had a better understanding of SRH and safe sexual practices than those in the younger age groups. Those who were sexually active had a better understanding of SRHR. However, the age of sexual debut varied considerably among countries. In the USA, most young people became sexually active before the age of 19, while in India and Nigeria, the age of sexual debut was much later. These differences were largely due to cultural beliefs regarding abstinence before marriage.

"Yes, I am aware of birth control and abortion pills. I have had two early abortions. Both pregnancies happened accidentally. I had sex with strangers while heavily drunk."

A 24-year-old sexually active female bisexual in the USA

Youth in the US and Mexico had more than three to four sexual partners. In contrast, young participants from India and Nigeria reported fewer sexual partners, typically ranging from none to a maximum of two.

"I have been sexually involved with four partners in the past, and I am currently dating. I am aware of condom use, which is a protective measure. I am aware of abstinence, which is also a protective measure. I feel it's important to not just fear pregnancy, but to also fear sexually transmitted diseases. Unsafe sex can lead to sexually transmitted diseases in males and females."

A 22-year-old sexually active male in Nigeria

Sources of information regarding SRH

When asked about their sources of information on SRH, youth across Mexico, India, the USA, and Nigeria identified primary and secondary sources. Primary sources included school curricula, social campaigns, HIV-focused campaigns, friends, family, and peers. Secondary sources of information were TV, advertisements, social media pages, the internet, and NGOs. In the US, consultation with healthcare providers and discussions with older siblings were also identified as important sources of information.

In both the US and Mexico, open discussions about SRH within families, schools, and universities played a significant role in reducing associated stigma. This openness contributed to a more comprehensive understanding of SRH among young people in these countries.

In Nigeria, while young people were engaged in discussions about SRH, their knowledge was primarily related to HIV and other sexually transmitted infections (STIs). This was because this information was provided by HIV campaigns. Although SRH topics were included in the school curriculum, young people in both Nigeria and India showed limited understanding, suggesting that the presence of SRH in the curriculum alone was insufficient. In India and Nigeria, the promotion of SRH knowledge was heavily influenced by how openly SRH topics were discussed. Social stigma around SRH inhibited open conversation and limited young people's access to accurate and comprehensive information. A 20-year-old sexually inactive heterosexual high school girl from India reflected, *"We have a chapter in the 10th standard about sexual health, but our teachers are not open to discussing it."* This highlights challenges faced by young people in India where even though SRH is a part of the formal education curriculum, the reluctance of teachers to openly discuss sexuality limits information received by youth.

Young people from all four countries, irrespective of age, mentioned the importance of obtaining information online. Youth in the US and Mexico also consulted healthcare professionals. Only highly qualified college graduates from India and Nigeria mentioned consulting healthcare professionals.

Pregnancy and abortion

Two major SRH concerns that can place females at risk for unsafe sexual behavior are pregnancy and abortion. When asked about their understanding of these topics, perceptions varied among high school students and college graduates. High school students in Nigeria and India had limited knowledge about abortion methods. *"I know there are some techniques of abortion, but I don't know exactly how they work."* High school students in Mexico were informed about condom use in school, but they still had unwanted pregnancies and abortions because they did not behave responsibly. High school students in India did not know about abortion.

"There are many unwanted pregnancies due to lack of awareness and responsibility."

A sexually active 18-year-old high school boy in Mexico

Unwanted pregnancy emerged as a significant issue among youth, particularly teenage pregnancies in the USA. Although both high school students and college graduates reported using birth control, they did not have a comprehensive understanding of the methods that led to unintended pregnancies and abortions. Attitudes toward abortion varied among young people. Some believed that abortion was appropriate but only in specific circumstances, such as during early sexual activity.

"It's a very complicated subject and there are a lot of things going on that people don't know about. I don't really know enough about it. I need to do more research. Yes, I will consult my parents and a doctor "

A 23-year-old sexually inactive male heterosexual in the USA

In Nigeria, high school students had misconceptions about unwanted pregnancies and self-managed abortions. They believed that alcohol, salt intake, and water could be used to terminate a pregnancy. This lack of knowledge led some girls to use incorrect or harmful medications. Fear of pregnancy drove some high school girls to seek advice from unqualified practitioners, which proved to be harmful. Abortion is illegal in Nigeria. Abortion can be performed by a legal, medical practitioner only if the woman's life is in danger. In fact, not only is abortion illegal in Nigeria, but it is also against their religious and cultural beliefs.

Abortion, particularly for self-managed abortion, remains a highly debated topic in the USA. Youth in the USA are not able to access safe abortion care in several states. Even though abortion is legal in India and some states in Mexico, it is associated with social stigma. High school students in Mexico admitted that they had limited knowledge about birth control. There were many unwanted pregnancies due to the lack of sex education. In India and Nigeria, young people hesitated to openly discuss the problem of abortion, which forced them to self-manage abortion with limited knowledge. Abortion is a sensitive topic and is associated with stigma. Young people had limited information about the use of abortion pills. High school students and college graduates from all four countries were aware of self-managed pregnancies.

Perceptions and usage of self-care interventions for SRH

In order to gauge youths' perceptions of self-care for SRH, high school students and college graduates were asked about their understanding of self-care, as well as their sources of information regarding contraceptive methods, unwanted pregnancies, abortion, post-abortion care, self-testing kits, self-sampling STI kits, and lubricants. In all four countries, responses were largely influenced by whether or not they had used the products.

Knowledge of self-care interventions for SRH

Across the four countries, young people's knowledge of contraception was generally limited to the use of condoms by males to prevent pregnancy and sexually transmitted infections (STIs). However, there were notable differences in the level of awareness between the genders and among young people from different regions. For example, in India, girl's knowledge about self-care interventions was limited to menstrual hygiene. However, in the USA, college graduates understood the importance of safe sex practices.

In Mexico, girls had a higher level of awareness and understanding of self-care products for birth control and abortion management compared to their male counterparts. Girls were more aware of the side-effects of various contraceptives. Boy's knowledge of contraception was limited to condoms. This shows that young girls in Mexico had a broader understanding of the range of available contraceptives.

In Nigeria, young people were educated about safe sex practices and the use of over-the-counter contraceptive methods, mainly condoms and birth control pills. Despite this, schools predominantly promoted abstinence as the most effective contraceptive method for unmarried students. High school students were aware that they could access condoms and birth control pills from local pharmacies. A 24-year-old sexually active college graduate from Mexico who had a preference for condoms said, *"Compared to other products, I feel condoms are much better as they are used externally."*

Gender differences and cultural contexts shaped young people's perceptions and usage of self-care interventions for SRH.

Practice and accessibility of self-care interventions

Youth had varied perspectives on the types of SRH interventions that they could use. College graduates demonstrated higher contraceptive use than high school students. Condom was the most frequently used contraceptive method by sexually active college graduates from all countries. Birth control pills were the next most commonly used method.

"I used it in the past and didn't like the fact it was causing headaches and mood swings. I will never use it. It can cause a lot of complications like blood clots."

A sexually active heterosexual female in the USA

US college graduates mentioned using at least one contraceptive method. They were aware of three to four contraceptive methods. College graduates, as well as high school students in Mexico, were aware of most of the contraceptive methods, including hormonal implants, birth control pills, female condoms, abstinence, IUDs, over-the-counter emergency contraception, and patches. High school students, however, mainly used condoms as they were easily available. They also used birth control pills. They were, however, afraid of their side-effects and the fact that they could cause hormonal imbalance. They also mentioned having difficulty in obtaining over-the-counter hormonal contraceptives.

College graduates from Nigeria had some knowledge of contraceptive methods but did not know how to use them. The majority of the girls were aware of over-the-counter hormonal contraceptives but did not like to use them. They preferred condoms over birth control pills because condoms were more affordable and accessible.

Youth in India knew about male condoms, female condoms, and birth control pills. They did not, however, know about self-injectables and contraceptive vaginal rings. Their knowledge of long-term contraceptive methods was limited or absent. Even married women did not have this knowledge.

For other self-care interventions, such as pregnancy kits, usage was governed by accessibility. High school students and college graduates were aware of self-testing pregnancy kits. Young people in the USA knew about self-testing kits for STIs, HIV and self-sampling kits for HPV. Special campaigns provided opportunities for youth in the US and Mexico to learn about HPV self-sampling and STI self-testing kits, which was not the case in India and Nigeria. People living with HIV in India were aware of self-testing kits but did not have access to them. Youth in Nigeria were aware of HIV and STIs but were not aware of self-testing kits. Knowledge about PEP and PrEP was limited in all four countries. Only medical graduates had this information.

The practice of using sanitary pads was universal. However, understanding of other products like menstrual cups and tampons was limited. Youth discussed factors that contributed to a lack of knowledge and awareness of menstrual products. Additionally, they expressed hesitation in trying new products due to uncertainty about their ingredients. And they did not know how to use them correctly. When youth in India were asked about the importance of SRH, they associated it with menstrual hygiene.

"We were taught about periods in sixth standard at school and were asked to use sanitary napkins. I faced extreme pain and felt uneasy. But I still use them."
A 19-year-old sexually inactive heterosexual female college graduate in India

Motivating factors in adopting self-care practices

When attempting to adopt self-care practices, many participants described self-care and overall wellbeing as the primary factors that motivated them to engage in these behaviors. Young people underscored the importance of self-care for physical, mental, and spiritual health. Self-care practices were, however, influenced by various other factors including ease of usage, cost, effectiveness, availability, accessibility, side-effects, privacy, stigma, and cultural taboos. For most young people, the role of education in informing them about self-care at a very young age was important in promoting self-care practices. Promoting healthy social norms and reducing stigma motivated young people to adopt self-care practices.

A high number of adolescents were sexually active in high school in the USA and Mexico. These sexually active students primarily used condoms, which were more readily available and affordable as compared to other contraceptives. As youth aged, they experimented with other contraceptives, such as over-the-counter hormonal contraceptives, lubricants, and self-testing kits. These had higher usage in the USA compared to Mexico and significantly higher usage when compared to India and Nigeria.

"I used an IUD as contraception is paid for by insurance "
                    A 26-year-old sexually active female bisexual in Mexico

In Mexico, college graduates used self-care interventions such as menstrual products, lubricants, and abortion pills. The fact that these products were easily available in stores, pharmacies, and online platforms without requiring a prescription facilitated their use. In India, participants indicated that the decision to use emergency contraception and lubricants was influenced by product quality and the preference of both partners.

In addition to the above-mentioned motivating factors, young people emphasized the importance of support networks and knowledge in overcoming demotivating factors related to reproductive health and trusted healthcare consultants over their parents when facing such issues. However, these experiences were primarily shared by youth from the USA and Mexico.

"I guess we would go to the medical system first because we trust it the most. We

generally avoid talking to our parents first."

A 23-year-old sexually active male heterosexual in the USA

Barriers to accessing self-care products

In order to understand the barriers in adopting self-care, we asked several questions like *"reasons for not using a particular self-care intervention"*, *"how to adopt and advance self-care"*, and *"the importance of self-care interventions"*. In response, many study participants said that there were several factors that demotivated them in accessing self-care products. These included social, economic, and cultural barriers, lack of accessibility, health emergencies like the COVID-19 pandemic, and gender.

Socioeconomic background

Socioeconomic factors significantly influenced the decision-making process regarding the adoption of self-care interventions. Young people who were socially and economically dependent on their families had difficulty. In India and Nigeria, youth up to the age of 23 years were financially dependent on their families. Girls were dependent on their parents and their partners. This limited their freedom to make independent decisions and posed a significant challenge.

Furthermore, when participants were asked about the challenges they faced in accessing self-care interventions, cost and lack of information about products emerged as major reasons affecting accessibility. This was a universal concern across all age groups in all four countries. Use of products like self-testing kits for HIV, self-sampling kits for STIs, and self-management of pregnancies and abortions was affected by these challenges.

In India, the study revealed that high school students of similar age but with different social and educational backgrounds had varied understandings of SRH. High school students from higher social classes and private educational institutions had greater awareness of SRH than students from public educational institutions with weaker socioeconomic backgrounds. Young people in India said that they could not watch TV programs about sexual life in front of their parents. They mentioned facing stigma within their families and found it uncomfortable to discuss sexual health matters with family members. Most girls shared their ideas about reproductive health with their mothers but these discussions were not related to sex.

Youth in the USA felt privileged as they did not face any social barriers while accessing self-care products for SRH. They did, however, faced financial constraints due to high cost, lack of insurance coverage, the need for prescriptions, and discrimination at healthcare facilities based on gender identity and sexual orientation.

Cultural and religious norms

Cultural and religious barriers limited young people's understanding of sexuality. Youth from Mexico, India, and Nigeria said that religious and cultural teachings impacted their level of awareness regarding SRH. For example, in Mexico, college graduates who studied at Catholic schools did not receive information on SRH through their schools. There were disparities in the quality and comprehensiveness of sex education provided in religious and conservative environments, creating unsafe spaces for young people to access self-care products and putting many of them at risk.

In Mexico, college graduates were able to obtain self-care products such as contraceptives and self-sampling kits, which were available in the market and at pharmacies. However, stigma, especially among women and girls, hindered their accessibility. Stigma affected their behaviors towards accessing and using self-care products.

In Nigeria, abortion is illegal and is against religious and cultural beliefs. There are major concerns regarding unwanted pregnancies. Youth discussed cultural beliefs surrounding the use of contraceptives, which ultimately affect women's sexual and reproductive health. Even the use of contraceptives is considered a taboo in Nigeria.

The influence of gender

Our study showed that gender significantly influenced SRH decision-making. Participants in Mexico, India, the USA, and Nigeria shared diverse opinions when asked about their experiences while engaging in sex with their partners. Opinions were polarized with strong agreements and disagreements. College graduates in the USA and Mexico were mindful of their partners' SRH. They understood the importance of obtaining consent from their partners and were concerned about their partners' sexual needs. Both boys and girls took equal responsibility for their SRH individually and within the relationship. However, there was some concern about the limited options available to females. There was a perception that women bear greater responsibility due to the nature of birth control methods.

There was less consensus among sexually active young people on statements like "*It is easy to talk about sex with a partner*" and "*You can tell your partner if you do not want to have sex.*" This was particularly true for unmarried girls in India, sexually active college graduates in Mexico, and high school students, both male and female, in the USA and Nigeria. For statements like "*Use a method to prevent pregnancy,*" there was a strong agreement among sexually active youth across all countries.

In Mexico, high school girls were better informed about sexual health matters than boys of the same age. Boys were allowed to go out alone and on trips, sometimes without permission, as they entered their teenage years when they were found to engage in risky sexual behavior.

In India, high school students from advantaged backgrounds were generally allowed to go out with parental supervision, regardless of gender.

However, girls from less economically advantaged backgrounds had fewer opportunities to go out than boys. College graduates, particularly those living independently, enjoyed greater freedom.

Females in Nigeria, including married women, were required to obtain permission from older family members or spouses to go out and spend time with their friends. Most of them had to return home by the evening. They were not allowed to stay out at night or consume alcohol or any other substance.

"I have experienced physical and sexual violence. My younger sister suffered sexual violence. She did not know who raped her until she was taken to the hospital, where she bled to death."

A 22-year-old sexually active male in Nigeria

Pandemics/ health emergencies like COVID-19

Participants shared that the COVID-19 pandemic had significantly impacted their lifestyles, daily routines, physical activities, and self-care practices. It posed a major challenge as it disrupted their way of life. Young people faced challenges in maintaining social distance and limiting social interaction. The pandemic increased their reliance on social media as a tool for staying connected. They had limited sexual activity, which contributed to anxiety and mental health issues. This experience was common among study participants in all four countries.

The pandemic created a stressful situation in healthcare facilities due to patient overload, inadequate services for other illnesses, and a shortage of medical staff. This was a greater problem for youth in Nigeria and India compared to those in Mexico and the USA.

Accessing healthcare facilities formally was a significant challenge, leading many young people to adopt self-care practices at home. Fear of infection was the universal reason for avoiding healthcare facilities and adopting self-care measures. However, practicing self-care, including physical activities like yoga, meditation, and exercise, could not help in some cases and led to anxiety and depression for those who were otherwise engaged in various activities during normal times. Sexually active young people who were living together or were married faced no difficulties in accessing contraceptives and other self-care interventions for SRH.

This comparative study underscores the importance of providing culturally sensitive, inclusive, and comprehensive SRH education to young people. SRH education programs should acknowledge the diverse realities and challenges faced by young people in different contexts. The approach to SRH education should go beyond providing basic knowledge on contraception. It should effectively promote young people's sexual and reproductive health and rights.

Our study sheds light on the critical gaps in knowledge, accessibility, and social support for young people during pregnancy and abortion across countries. In order to increase the engagement of young people, efforts should focus on improving the accessibility of self-care products, fostering open communication about SRH, and creating a supportive environment. Efforts should be made to destigmatize conversations around SRH, particularly on abortion, by promoting open dialogue and offering non-judgmental services to young people.

References

1. Allan J & Thompson A. Experiences of young people and their carers with a rural mobile mental health support service: A qualitative study. International Journal of Environmental Research and Public Health. 2023 Jan 18;20(3):1774. https://www.ncbi.nlm.nih.gov/pmc/articles/PMC9914613/

2. Koop A. Mapping the world's youngest and oldest countries. Visual Capitalist. 2021 Feb 12. https://www.visualcapitalist.com/worlds-youngest-and-oldest-countries/#google_vignette

3. Y+ Global. Self-care: Young People Taking Control! Y+ Global. https://w

ww.yplusglobal.org/projects-self-care-young-people-taking-control

4. World Health Organization. Self-care for health and well-being. World Health Organization. https://www.who.int/health-topics/self-care

5. Self-care for Trailblazer Group. Self-Care: For youth, by youth. PSI. 2021 May 21. https://www.psi.org/project/self-care/self-care-for-youth-by-you th/, https://www.psi.org/project/self-care/self-care-for-youth-by-youth/

6. Y+ Global. Put yourself first and the power of self-care. Young people highlight the importance of self-care and its benefits after a month-long campaign. Y+ Global. https://www.yplusglobal.org/www.yplusglobal.org

The Way Forward

A sh Pachauri, Director, Center for Human Progress, New Delhi, India, and Senior Mentor, POP (Protect Our Planet) Movement, New York, USA

Saroj Pachauri, Public Health Specialist, Trustee, Center for Human Progress, New Delhi, India, and Director, POP (Protect Our Planet) Movement, New York, USA

The self-care experiences of high school students and college graduates across diverse regions such as Mexico, India, the USA, and Nigeria highlight self-care interventions' critical role in promoting sexual and reproductive health and rights (SRHR). As we move forward, we must systematically implement self-care interventions, integrating them into mainstream healthcare systems to achieve Universal Health Coverage (UHC) and the Sustainable Development Goals (SDGs).

Key actions and recommendations:

1. Policy and framework development

- Governments and health organizations should develop comprehensive policies and frameworks supporting self-care interventions. These should align with WHO guidelines and prioritize SRHR.

2. Education and awareness

- Education and awareness programs to address sociocultural barriers, misinformation, and stigma associated with self-care practices should be enhanced. Tailored educational initiatives can empower young people with knowledge and autonomy over their health choices.

3. Technology integration

- Mobile health (m-health) technologies must be leveraged to improve access to self-care services. Mobile platforms can provide reliable information, facilitate self-testing, and offer telehealth consultations, particularly in underserved regions.

4. Gender-sensitive approaches

- Gender-sensitive approaches should be implemented to address the unique challenges faced by different genders. This includes ensuring equitable access to self-care resources and addressing gender-specific health concerns.

5. Research and data collection:

- Extensive research should be conducted to fill the gaps in knowledge regarding self-care practices among youth. Data-driven insights are essential for developing targeted interventions and monitoring the effectiveness of self-care strategies.

6. Supportive environments

- Supportive environments should be created to encourage the adoption of self-care practices. These include fostering community support, reducing legal barriers, and ensuring confidentiality and privacy in health services.

7. Collaboration and partnerships

- Collaboration should be forged among governments, non-governmental organizations, healthcare providers, and technology firms to create synergistic efforts that enhance the reach and impact of self-care interventions.

Emphasizing the importance of self-care in light of the COVID-19 pandemic

The COVID-19 pandemic has dramatically underscored the importance of self-care, revealing both vulnerabilities and opportunities within global healthcare systems. As healthcare resources became increasingly strained, individuals' need to manage aspects of their health independently became more urgent. The pandemic highlighted several key areas where self-care can significantly contribute to public health and resilience against future crises.

Enhanced resilience and autonomy: Self-care empowers individuals to take proactive steps in managing their health, reducing dependency on overburdened healthcare systems. During the pandemic, self-care practices such as self-testing, self-isolation, and remote health monitoring became crucial in managing the spread of the virus and ensuring timely treatment. By promoting self-care, individuals can develop greater resilience and autonomy, enabling them to respond effectively to health challenges.

Reduced healthcare burden: The influx of COVID-19 patients overwhelmed many healthcare facilities, leading to routine and preventive care delays. Self-care interventions, such as managing chronic conditions at home, using telemedicine services, and adhering to prescribed self-medication protocols, helped alleviate some of this burden. Encouraging self-care can thus free up critical healthcare resources, allowing healthcare professionals to focus on more severe cases and emergencies.

Continuity of care: Lockdowns and social distancing measures disrupted regular healthcare services, making it difficult for many to access essential health services. Self-care practices ensured the continuity of care for numerous individuals, particularly those with chronic conditions or those requiring regular medication. Integrating self-care into everyday health routines allows individuals to maintain their health and wellbeing even when traditional healthcare services are disrupted.

Mental health and wellbeing: The psychological impact of the pandemic has been profound, with increased levels of anxiety, depression, and stress reported globally. Self-care practices, including mindfulness, exercise, and healthy lifestyle choices, are vital for mental health and wellbeing. Promoting mental health self-care can help individuals manage stress and anxiety, improving their overall quality of life during challenging times.

Accessibility and equity: The pandemic exposed significant health inequities, particularly in underserved and marginalized communities. Self-care interventions can bridge gaps in healthcare access by providing low-cost, scalable solutions that reach a broader population. Mobile health technologies and community-based self-care programs can be crucial in delivering health services to those otherwise excluded from the formal healthcare system.

Preparedness for future crises: Building robust self-care practices is essential for preparedness against future health crises. Educating and equipping individuals with the knowledge and tools to manage their health can create a more resilient population capable of withstanding health emergencies. This preparedness not only benefits individuals but also strengthens public health systems overall.

In conclusion, the COVID-19 pandemic has highlighted the critical importance of self-care in maintaining health and wellbeing amidst unprecedented challenges. As we move forward, integrating self-care into public health strategies will be essential for creating a resilient, equitable, and efficient healthcare system capable of responding to current and future health crises. Promoting self-care is not just a temporary solution but a sustainable approach to achieving long-term health outcomes and universal health coverage.

Conclusion

The COVID-19 pandemic has starkly illuminated the critical role of self-care in maintaining health and resilience amidst unprecedented pressures on global healthcare systems. As we navigate the path forward, we must systematically integrate self-care interventions into mainstream healthcare frameworks to achieve Universal Health Coverage (UHC) and the Sustainable Development Goals (SDGs).

Key actions include developing comprehensive policies, enhancing education and awareness, leveraging mobile health technologies, adopting gender-sensitive approaches, conducting extensive research, creating supportive environments, and fostering collaboration among key stakeholders. These measures are foundational to ensuring that self-care becomes a sustainable and integral part of public health strategies.

The pandemic has demonstrated that self-care empowers individuals, re-duces the burden on healthcare systems, ensures continuity of care, supports mental health and wellbeing, enhances accessibility and equity, and prepares populations for future health crises. By promoting self-care, individuals can take proactive steps in managing their health, reducing dependency on overburdened healthcare systems and building greater resilience and autonomy.

The systematic implementation of self-care interventions is not merely a temporary response to challenges posed by the COVID-19 pandemic but a sustainable and forward-looking approach to public health and health crisis preparedness. By embracing self-care, we can create a more resilient, equitable, and efficient healthcare system that ensures better health outcomes for all, now and in the future.

By focusing on these actions, we can significantly improve the sexual and reproductive health outcomes of young people globally. Systematic implementation of self-care interventions, supported by robust policies, education, technology, and research, will pave the way for healthier, empowered, and informed youth, contributing to the overall goal of Universal Health Coverage.

Acronyms

This section provides a comprehensive list of acronyms used throughout the book to ensure readers' clarity and ease of reference. Familiarity with these abbreviations will enhance understanding of the topics discussed and facilitate smoother reading. Acronyms are listed in alphabetical order for quick access.

AAP: American Academy of Pediatrics

AFR: Adolescent Fertility Rate

ASHA: Accredited Social Health Activist

AYP: Adolescent and Young People

BMJ: British Medical Journal

CAP: Condom Availability Program

CDC: Centers for Disease Control

CIIEMAD: Centro Interdisciplinario de Investigaciones y Estudios Sobre Medio Ambiente y Desarrollo

CSE: Comprehensive Sexuality Education

FDA: Food and Drug Administration

FGD: Focus Group Discussion

FSW: Female Sex Worker

HIV: Human Immunodeficiency Virus

HIVST: Human Immunodeficiency Virus Self-Testing

HPV: Human Papilloma Virus

IDI: In-Depth Interviews

IMIFAP: Mexican Institute of Family and Population Research

IPN: Instituto Politécnico Nacional

IRB: Institutional Review Board

IUD: Intrauterine Device

LGBTQ+: Lesbian, Gay, Bisexual, Transgender, Queer or Questioning

LMIC: Low- and Middle-Income Countries

MMR: Maternal Mortality Ratio

MMR: Maternal Mortality Rate

MSM: Men who have Sex with Men

MTP: Medical Termination of Pregnancy

NFHS: National Family Health Survey

NSFG: National Survey of Family Growth

OECD: Organization for Economic Co-operation and Development

PMC: PubMed Central

POCSO: Protection of Children from Sexual Offences

POP Movement: Protect Our Planet Movement

PrEP: Pre-Exposure Prophylaxis

PTSD: Post-Traumatic Stress Disorder

RKSK: *Rashtriya Kishor Swasthya Karyakram*

SDG: Sustainable Development Goals

SEP: Mexican Ministry of Public Education

SRH: Sexual and Reproductive Health

SRHR: Sexual and Reproductive Health and RightsSTDs Sexually Transmitted Diseases

STI: Sexually Transmitted Infection

UHC: Universal Health Coverage

UNAM: Universidad Nacional Autónoma de México

UNFPA: United Nations Fund for Population Activities

UNICEF: United Nations International Children's Emergency Fund

WHO: World Health Organization

YRBSS: Youth Risk Behavior Surveillance System

Profile of Contributors

Dr. Saroj Pachauri, Public Health Specialist, Trustee, Center for Human Progress, New Delhi, India, and Director, POP (Protect Our Planet) Movement, New York, USA

As a public health physician, Dr. Pachauri has been extensively engaged with research on family planning, maternal and child health, sexual and reproductive health and rights, HIV and AIDS, and poverty, gender and youth. In 1996, she joined as Regional Director, South and East Asia, Population Council and established its regional office in New Delhi which she managed until 2014. In 2011, she was awarded the prestigious title of Distinguished Scholar, an honor rarely bestowed.

She worked with the Ford Foundation's New Delhi Office (1983-1994) and supported child survival, women's health, sexual and reproductive health, and HIV and AIDS programs. Before that, she worked with the International Fertility Research Program (IFRP) which was later renamed Family Health International (1971-1975) and the India Fertility Research Programme (1975-1983). She designed and monitored multi-centric clinical trials globally to assess the safety and effectiveness of fertility control technologies. During 1962-1971, as faculty of the Departments of Preventive and Social Medicine at the Lady Hardinge Medical College, New Delhi and the Institute of Medicine Sciences, Varanasi, she helped to develop this new discipline.

She has published twelve books and contributed chapters to 20 books. She has over 100 publications in peer-reviewed journals and several articles in print media.

Dr. Ash Pachauri, Director, Center for Human Progress, New Delhi, India, and Senior Mentor, POP (Protect Our Planet) Movement, New York, USA

Dr. Ash Pachauri has a PhD in behavioral science and technology and a master's in international management. Having worked with McKinsey & Company before pursuing a career in the social development arena, Dr. Pachauri's experience in public health and sustainable development emerges from a range of initiatives. Notably, he has made significant contributions to the Bill & Melinda Gates Foundation by contributing to its public health and community agenda, the UN by focusing on youth, health, and the Sustainable Development Goals (SDGs), and the Center for Disease Control program interventions in the US by focusing on community interventions, especially for vulnerable youth. He has also been instrumental in founding and building the POP Movement and the World Sustainable Development Forum. He is a technical adviser to the World Health Organization on Self-Care Global Guidelines to support youth, communities, and global governments.

Dr. Pachauri has been a pioneer in the use of information technology for development. His innovative approaches have been key to spearheading community—and youth-led self-care interventions, leading to global capacity building and adoption of self-care among youth. As a master trainer in behavior change communications and strategic leadership, Dr. Pachauri has led over 20,000 workshops, events, and global outreach to youth and communities to promote global health and climate action.

Widely published, winner of the prestigious Overseas Research Scholarship, awarded for advanced studies in the U.K., and recognized for his academic achievements, Dr. Pachauri's awards and recognitions reflect his significant contributions to the field. The United Nations has recognized Dr. Pachauri for his dedication and leadership in their flagship publication, "Portraits of Commitment," A testament to his influence in the field. In 2021, he was awarded the GlobalMindED Inclusive Leadership Award for action in Energy and Sustainability, a recognition of his commitment to inclusive and sustainable development among young people worldwide. He is an Associate Fellow of the World Academy of Art and Science, a position that underscores his academic standing. Dr. Pachauri serves on the Boards and Advisory groups of several organizations and initiatives worldwide, including the global movement on bone health, the Climate Change Coalition, and the Global Union of Scientists for Peace. He demonstrates leadership and influence in the global health and climate action community.

Dra. Norma Patricia Muñoz-Sevilla, Centro Interdisciplinario de Investigaciones y Estudios Sobre Medio Ambiente y Desarrollo (CIIEMAD), Instituto Politécnico Nacional (IPN), México

Dra Norma studied Biology at the National School of Biological Sciences (Escuela Nacional de Ciencias Biológicas - ENCB) of the National Polytechnic Institute (Instituto Politécnico Nacional, IPN) and graduated in 1982. She obtained her Doctorate in Biological Oceanography at the Université d 'Aix-Marseille II, France and a post-doctorate in Marine Biochemistry at the École Pratique des Hautes Études in Paris in 1990. She is a Member of National System of Researchers (Sistema Nacional de Investigadores - SNI Level II) of the National Council for Humanities and Technological Sciences [Consejo Nacional de Humanidades Ciencias y Tecnologías (CONAHCYT)].

She has trained in human resources at the postgraduate, Masters and Doctorate level at the Interdisciplinary Center of Marine Sciences, Interdisciplinary Research Center for Regional Integral Development, Sinaloa Unit, Center for Research and Advanced Studies, Mérida Unit, the Center Interdisciplinary Research and Studies in Environment and Development and the National Polytechnic Institute. She has supervised 30 masters in science and 12 doctorate students. She taught postgraduate courses at the IPN and was a Conference Teacher at École Pratique des Hautes Études in Concarneau,

France.

She has been director and/or participant in 59 projects related to the management of marine resources, coastal development, water resources, marine pollution, environmental impact, and integral management of the coastal zone among others while she worked in the National Polytechnic Institute (IPN), National Council for Humanities and Technological Sciences [Consejo Nacional de Humanidades Ciencias y Tecnologías (CONAHCYT)] and other national and international organizations. She has published 89 scientific articles, 18 chapters in books and three books on coastal zones and environmental deterioration.

She has been Advisor to the Secretariat of the Environment and Natural Resources of Mexico in matters of oceans and coasts for more than 10 years, external advisor to international organizations such as the United Nations Educational, Scientific and Cultural Organization (UNESCO), the United Nations Environment Programme (UNEP), the United Nations (UN), and the United Nations Industrial Development Organizations (UNIDO) for marine planning, integrated coastal management, and capacity building in Latin America in the coastal zone, governance of the Gulf of Mexico, coastal continental water, and public policies among others. She has received approximately 41 awards for her professional performance including a distinction from the American Biographical Institute as Great Woman of the 21 Century 2004/2005 edition in the area of sustainable development. The Order of the Academic Palms in the degree of Knight. Decoration was awarded to her by the Government of the French Republic in 2011. She received an Honorable Mention in the Doctorate in Biological Oceanography of the University of Aix-Marseille II in France. A Diploma of Honor was awarded by the University of Los Andes, Venezuela for her outstanding academic career and she was recognized by the Polytechnic Women Leaders 2022.

Ms. Komal Mittal, Research Associate, Center for Human Progress, New Delhi, India and Youth Mentor, POP (Protect Our Planet) Movement, New

York, USA

Komal Mittal is a Research Associate at the Center for Human Progress. She is also a Global Youth Mentor with the POP Movement. She has conducted extensive research on understanding self-care practices of the most marginalized and vulnerable communities in India. This research was supported by the World Health Organization (WHO). She led a national youth group supported by the Joint United Nations Programme on HIV/AIDS. This program focused on promoting leadership and advocacy for the Sustainable Development Goals.

Komal has been a proactive participant, as also, an organizer for several national and international conferences and has presented many research papers and reports on public health and climate issues. She was awarded the 'Research Excellence Award' in the field of biotechnology for her study on 'Extraction of Acid Soluble Collagen from Soybean and Tomato'. She co-authored a book entitled "Sexual and Reproductive Health and Rights: Self-care for Achieving Universal Health Coverage" with Dr. Saroj Pachauri and Dr. Ash Pachauri. This book was published by Springer Publishers in 2020. With a focus on working on mental health, she contributed her expertise to uncover the vulnerability of human life and sustenance. This research aims to understand how diverse population groups and people who are ostracized were dealt with the deprivation of basic human rights and health services especially during the COVID-19 pandemic.

She committed herself to preserve the environment and protect our planet. She believes in providing education and empowering communities, building awareness about environmental and health issues, and promoting youth and community action for improving the quality of life. She reaches out to young leaders from the disadvantaged sections of society with a message of 'action' by deploying her leadership skills, perseverance, commitment, and enthusiasm for a better and sustainable tomorrow.

Ms. Drishya Pathak, Research Associate, Center for Human Progress, New Delhi, India and Youth Mentor, POP (Protect Our Planet) Movement, New York, USA

Drishya Pathak is a public health professional with seven years of experience in the public health and development sectors. She completed her Masters Degree in Health Management from the International Institute of Health Management and Research in 2019 and her undergraduate degree in Microbiology from the University of Delhi. She has presented several reports in the area of public health. She supported the planning, implementation, and documentation of the Second World Sustainable Development Forum in Durango, México in 2020.

Drishya is currently a Research Associate with the Center for Human Progress. She is working on projects on the sexual and reproductive health needs of key populations and people living with HIV (PLHIV). She has hands-on experience of working closely on issues like acudetox, education and awareness, and gender empowerment. She was involved with the implementation and training for the Integrated Digital Adherence Technology (IDAT) Project on Tuberculosis. She approaches environmental sciences through a public health lens as demonstrated in her recent work on 'Leaching of Chemicals from Plastic Food Contact Materials into Food', which was recognized on an international platform.

Ms. Philo Magdalene Antony Samy, Communications and Research Assistant, Center for Human Progress, New Delhi, India, and Global Youth Mentor, POP (Protect Our Planet) Movement, New York, USA

Philo Magdalene is a Youth Mentor at the POP Movement, where she directs communications and program management. She supported the implementation of the Second World Sustainable Development Forum in Durango in March 2020 and co-led the documentation process. Philo is also a Research Analyst at the Center for Human Progress where she supported the advancement of the living WHO Consolidated Guideline on Self-Care Interventions for Sexual and Reproductive Health. Through CHP, she aided the Country Offices of UNAIDS and WHO and led the report writing and documentation of conferences focused on Universal Health Coverage and Sustainable Development Goals. In 2020, she received the AIDS 2020 Scholarship award and was selected to be the International AIDS Society Youth Ambassador from India for 2020 International AIDS Conference (Virtual).

Philo graduated with a Masters Degree in Literary and Cultural Studies from the English and Foreign Languages University, Hyderabad in 2021. An avid learner, she is intent on researching and understanding the interactions between development and the environment and its implications on marginal-izing different populations.

Ms. Nahid Perez Ayala, Medical Student and Youth Mentor, POP (Protect Our Planet) Movement, New York, USA

Nahid Perez Ayala is a medical student at the University of Monterrey and a climate activist. As a mentor for the POP Movement and YOUNGO, she had the opportunity to contribute in the area of Health and Climate Change. Nahid represented Mexico in major events such as COY16 and the British Embassy's Climate Boot Camp 2021.

Her research includes projects with World Health Organization on sexual and reproductive health among youth and a study on the health impacts of sargassum in the Mexican Caribbean. At her university, she presented a study on the epigenetics of students in the health field with elevated stress levels. As president of her student group, Nahid carried out blood donation campaigns, educational advisories for medical students, and book donation campaigns. She has also been the coordinator of the Heart Monterrey Cardiology Congress.

9 798330 507757